PURSUING
THE GOSPEL

PURSUING THE GOSPEL

Redeeming Evangelism in a Post-Christian Culture

MITCHELL S. JOHNSON

www.pursuingthegospel.com

PRAISE FOR PURSUING THE GOSPEL

"*Pursuing the Gospel* is relevant, revolutionary, and revealing for pastors, leaders, or any person who desires to better understand the current culture of Christianity. Mitchell weaves his personal journey into the message that the Gospel is good and it's for everybody. His sound words of wisdom will open your eyes to the reality of church culture and propel you to action for change. It's a must-read to have your thumb on the pulse of many millennial's hearts."

-Paula A. Lambert
Author of This Season of Hope,
This Season of Freedom

"I had the privilege of serving as the evangelism co-chairman for the 2016 Reinhard Bonnke Gospel Crusade in Atlanta, GA. In preparation for the event, we held a citywide youth rally with Evangelist Todd White, that gathered over 2,000 young people. The following day, we trained 800 evangelists in sharing the love of God through healing and prophetic activation before sending them out all over the metro area. When we reassembled that afternoon, many wonderful testimonies were shared of people meeting Jesus and getting healed. During the crusade, over 14,000 people filled the arena, with many experiencing salvation for the first time. Large events like this train us and stir the fire in us. But we can't let it stop there! Evangelism isn't a hat we take off when the stadium lights fade. It is a lifestyle. In *Pursuing the Gospel*, Mitchell encourages us to see each day as an opportunity to share the Gospel and invite people into God's family. He displaces common misnomers about evangelism and simplifies the act of telling people about Jesus. *Pursuing the Gospel* is great for the seasoned revivalist and the one just learning to share their faith. I recommend it as an evangelism training tool for churches and ministries."

-David Edwards
Director, Author of Activating a Prophetic Lifestyle,
The Call for Revivalists

"Do you have an urge deep down to share the love of Jesus with those around you, but have been turned off by how you've seen it done before? Are you nervous that it'll just feel like a sales pitch when you know this gift of salvation is the lifeline that we all need? This is why I'm thankful for Mitchell's book! None of us want to coerce those around us with pressure-filled words about heaven and hell. Mitchell's writing is a book sharpened by scripture and his own life's pursuit of sharing the Gospel. Take this tool and be empowered to see how God is already at work in the lives of everyone around you. Mitchell's highest challenge to us is obedience to God's voice when

He prompts us to speak to those around us. We do this best when we stay rooted in our own identities as children of God!"

-Haley Lamb
Founder at Made for this Gathering,
Board Member of Gospel for Latin America

"Mitchell does an amazing job of outlining the complex nature of witnessing while providing helpful ways for you and those you lead to be bold in your proclamation of Christ. This is a book saturated with a wealth of gold for those who want to better fulfill the great commission. I highly recommend it!"

-Jason Burton
Pastor of Wrens Church of God

ISBN: 9798618216562

Dedicated to Phillip and Alex
-I love the moments that Heaven touches Earth,
They give me hope that we're not that far from home...

.

CONTENTS

FOREWORD

The Gospel is Good News; It's not bad news with a positive twist. Its subject is Jesus, and humanity is the object He invites us into when we experience the transformative power of His goodness. The preaching of the Gospel is not just a task bestowed upon believers; it's the lifestyle of those who are truly convinced of the greatest act of love expressed to mankind. It will infiltrate our every facet of life and captivate our hearts. This message of love causes us to see others through the eyes of Jesus. The Gospel compels us to move.

My initial interaction with the preaching of the Gospel started as a child. I was a pastor's kid and involved in almost every aspect of ministry, from church services, to hosting tent revivals, and outside outreach campaigns. We were trained to be bold and to speak with authority. We were urged to win souls and pray prayers. That was all good. But we were never taught to build relationships. We weren't trained to show compassion or have regard for someone's life story. In my upbringing, we weren't taught to preach Christ's love, we were taught to love preaching. Ministry had become an idol that caused us to forget about loving Jesus and others well - sometimes even our own family.

When I entered college at Oral Roberts University, I was a broken young man. My parents divorced a couple of years earlier, and my brother had passed a week before I started at the school. I was hurting inside, but I had the call of God on my life and a scholarship, so I left for Tulsa. It was my first time living away from home, and I found myself completely lonely. I was scared, fractured, and desperate for a touch from God in my life. I also needed healthy human connection, so I joined an outreach team that served soup and hot chocolate to people at the local homeless shelter.

One evening during an outreach, we were asked to come inside the shelter and hang out with the homeless men. As I leaned against a wall in the sitting room, I discovered I was highly intimidated and at a loss for words. I saw people in need and had nothing to say. I felt sorry for them, but I was too afraid to interact. Passing out a cup of soup and saying, "God bless you" was easy compared to the need to have an actual conversation.

A homeless man named Roger called me over and told

me he wanted to go outside to speak with me alone. We went outside, and he leaned towards me and asked, "Are you a Christian?" I replied affirmatively. He said, "Then tell me something I need to know." I began to ask him a few shallow questions, and he soon realized how intimated I was. He said there was something about me he didn't like.

He commanded, "Take your hat off!" I took my hat off. He then said, "Put it back on." I put it back on. "Take it off, again." I quickly pulled my hat back off, timidly following his commands.

He said, "See, you're afraid, and that fear makes you fake. You have the truth inside of you, and love should make you want to share that truth. If you have the antidote to the disease that is destroying the world, why wouldn't you share it with me? But you couldn't even have a normal conversation with me." He then flagged a cab and rode away. I was left standing alone, ashamed, and burdened.

That night, in my dorm, I began crying out to God to heal my heart and teach me to love the way He loves. I asked Him to empower me with the Holy Spirit to be moved with compassion, and I asked Him to show me how to really love people. Little did I know, God was going to use an encounter with a homeless man named Roger to teach me how to desire freedom and love so I could become an authentic minister of the Gospel. Through fear and my own personal pain, I failed to realize that I had experienced the goodness of God so many times in my life. I neglected to see I had been empowered by a loving God who had saved me from all my transgressions. I'd forgotten I had a real-life story and a personal history with Jesus. My experiences with Him would call me to share the Truth to a real world about a real God. That experience with Roger changed my heart and perspective forever.

Years later, I have grown to value intimacy with God and authenticity in relationships above everything else I pursue. Knowing God in His goodness and loving others without agenda has been the driving force behind planting the church I pastor in Augusta, Georgia. I also serve as the executive director of a program for homeless men. I spend much of my time counseling and coaching them to grow into their full potential and to live in freedom. They are beat up, broken, and ashamed. My job is to introduce them to Jesus and share with them the beauty of the Gospel. My life and ministry have had a regeneration over the years. At one time, preaching the Gospel for me was about results and personal agenda. Now it's about an authentic process towards relationship with people who God loves abundantly.

This brings me to the reason I am writing this foreword.

I met Mitchell at a mutual friend's birthday dinner. Leading up to that moment, we had not officially met, but he had visited the church I pastor a few times. As the party was ending, we found ourselves talking to each other outside of the Mexican restaurant. I discovered a little about him, what he did for a living, and so forth. It was small talk, but we quickly decided to have a follow up chat to get to know each other better. We set up a time to connect a few weeks later.

The second time we connected, we met at a local Tex-Mex joint to eat. That time, we got to dive a little deeper with each other. That conversation fostered a bit of an inquisition. He was in the middle of a transition in life and ministry, and I asked a lot of questions. He was genuine, forthright, yet tactful in his interaction with me. He didn't know me, and I didn't know him. I could sense he was interested in sharing his heart and seeking to find a safe place to speak his mind, but he was also preserving and mindful - looking to be able to trust me. It's what we all long for - safety and authenticity so we can truly be ourselves through vulnerability.

This is the context and setting from which Mitchell writes *Pursuing the Gospel*. He is introducing us all to walk in the boldness of the Holy Spirit, while ensuring that our compassion for others is the forefront of how we preach the Good News. The text is entwined with Mitchell's history and experiences. It gives us insight into his own life's pursuit. He is inviting us all into the pursuit of being

Gospel-bearers by being responsible, accountable, and compassionate as we share the Good News. His own life is the backdrop for why it's important to become relational, safe, and empowered in evangelizing to a lost world. This book stays true to classical evangelicalism while presenting a refreshing approach on how to handle the message relationally.

God is calling us to become authentic in our pursuit and proclamation of the Gospel. He is calling us to become authentic in our pursuit of relationships with others, as well. Even Paul's charge to Pastor Timothy is to become a faithful and prudent carrier of Jesus' Gospel:

"But you, keep your head in all situations, endure hardship, do the work of an evangelist, discharge all the duties of your ministry."

-2 Timothy 4:5

Jesus is the desire of the nations and the answer to every fallen condition. He is the antidote to the disease of sin and the Truth to the lies of the enemy. The Good News is better than we can imagine. This is our time to become good and faithful stewards of the most impacting and important message that has ever been expressed. Mitchell invites us into this lifestyle in *Pursuing the Gospel*. It's a perspective I feel must be heard.

-Christopher S. Jones
Pastor/Founder, Father's House Augusta

INTRODUCTION

The year 2017 would prove to be a difficult one for me. With confidence I can say it was one of the hardest seasons of my life. I'd been in youth ministry for three years and had recently been given a great opportunity at a reputable church. My eyes were wide open with vision and possibility as this was the chance of a young minister's lifetime. I was exactly where I wanted, and frankly, where I felt I deserved to be. In my time there, I was very successful in my role. My youth ministry was growing, and I was building healthy relationships with the members of the church. I never thought it would come to an unexpected halt.

During the first week back after the new year, it happened. The church was entering a season of leadership transition, and we were all ready for whatever that looked like. As my new pastor called me into his office that Wednesday morning, I didn't expect that I would drive away hurt, angry and utterly broken only a short half-hour later. He released me from my position with little conversation or explanation. I was so hurt and confused. I wanted answers, but unfortunately, I never got them. I was in a brand-new city, without a job or family nearby. I did the only logical thing I could think of; I moved back home.

Two months later, I took a part-time staff position at a church in my hometown. I was still bitter, angry, and on a mission to prove to everyone that I wasn't a failure. My heart just wasn't healthy. The Lord placed me in the arms of a community of people who provided the healing I desperately needed. They helped me learn to sit in the fire to refine and purify my heart. I became a member of a family who graciously allowed me to see that I was pursuing things that carried no eternal weight. Numbers, status and position aren't as valuable in our callings as pursuing the heart of God, and those are the things I was after.

It was rough and emotional, but it was a monumental year of transformation. It's the year I grasped what it meant to pursue the Gospel.

Pursue has been my favorite word to use during my journey over the past couple of years. A question that I often realign myself with is, "What am I pursuing?" Am I going after the humility of Jesus and the heart of the Father, or am I slipping back into the desire to be successful and well known? It's been a humbling question that has allowed me to keep my motives pure.

Pursue, according to Webster, is to "follow someone or something to catch or attack." When I hear this word, I think of a lion's pursuit of catching his prey. When a lion wakes up, he knows his number one priority is to protect and provide for his family. As he seeks for food, he must be strategic in finding and making a kill worth eating. He stalks, hunts and waits for the perfect time to strike. If you have watched an episode of Animal Planet, this scene is familiar to you. What those tv shows don't show you is his relentlessness in waking up the next morning, just to do it all over again.

The Gospel isn't something that we catch just once. We must pursue it to catch it daily. The good news of Jesus impacts our lives every day. If we don't pursue it, it's easy to slip back into the motives of the flesh. We must pursue the Gospel because it's a love story worth always catching.

To catch the Gospel is to have a genuine revelation of Jesus. When we have a new revelation of who He is, we catch the power of the Gospel all over again. We are in a time where many people have caught the story of Jesus and eventually dropped it, only to pick up their duty of works instead. We can become so enthralled in working for our salvation, we forget to look to the beauty of the Gospel story that initially saved us.

After a lion makes the kill, he doesn't leave it there for the buzzards to devour. He takes it back to his pride and they feast. If he were to go back home with nothing, his family would wonder if he caught anything to begin with. He knows what he has caught will bring sustenance to his family. So, he values it, and he shares it.

I believe when you catch the beauty of the Gospel, you won't be able to help but share it with others. The Gospel that we carry will bring life to those around us. We must pursue and share it every day. I have been a "believer" my entire life, but I finally caught the Gospel in 2017. In response, a desire to see authentic evangelism has erupted inside of me. I've come from a place of pursuing my wants to pursuing the things in life that matter to the heart of God. Evangelism is the most vital one for me.

I wrote this book hoping you will become like the lion in his daily pursuit; to catch and share. There are many misconceptions about the Gospel and why Jesus died. We will explore many of these areas and some practicalities you can use to share the Gospel with more confidence.

You have everything that you need to share the story of Jesus with those around you. We overcome by the blood of the lamb and the word of our testimony. As followers of Jesus, we have both. When we understand the truth of the Gospel and how it changes us, we can't help but tell the world about this supernatural love.

Because I believe in the power of testimonies, I have included stories from people within my community at the end of several chapters. Be encouraged as you read through them and encounter the faith exuding from each one! These are powerful moments of evangelism and prophecy.

If you feel you haven't quite caught the Gospel or lack the equipping needed to share your story, this book is for you! I wouldn't be as enthusiastic to share it with you if it didn't transform my life first. Writing it has brought so much humility and adoration for the Lord to my heart. I offer my words and experience to you as a response to His gift of grace in my life.

The Gospel message inside of you is bursting at the seams. You are a powerful witness for the Lord, and you will become a selfless, humble and passionate carrier of the good news. God bless you on your journey in advancing the Gospel. May you always be ready to give an account for the hope that lives inside of you!

CHATROOM EVANGELISM

It was a Friday night. I was sitting in my dorm room with nothing to do. Speaking on the phone with a friend from home, he insisted we enter a chatroom and talk back and forth. This was long before smartphones and the social media outlets we have today.

I setup my account and logged in for the first time. I found my friend, and we chatted back and forth for a while. The time came for him to head to a movie, so we disconnected. I spent more time just browsing around the chatroom and ended up in a conversation with someone I didn't know. We introduced ourselves and found out a little more about each other. He was a 13-year-old teenage boy. In my mind I thought maybe I should just log off, but in my spirit, I felt a drawing to chat with him more.

We began having a small conversation. Rather quickly, he opened up to me and shared about his home life. He told me how he was made fun of and mistreated at school, and how he hated life. He believed no one cared for him. My heart broke, but immediately my spirit came alive and the good news of Jesus came forth. I shared with him about Jesus and how His love is perfect, even when we can't find it elsewhere.

We spoke for nearly 3 hours in that chatroom. There were moments of typed out prayer and sharing God's Word. He revealed to me deeper in our conversation that he was planning to end his life that night. He said he had a knife sitting right next to him. He logged-on one last time to see if there was anyone out there that really cared. What he learned that night was that Jesus cares for him. So much in fact, He'd use a stranger to communicate His love for him in such a helpless situation.

I gave him my email address, and a few days later received an email from his mother. She thanked me for that chatroom encounter. The boy shared everything that happened with her! It opened up vulnerable conversations between them and they even attended church that Sunday together as a family. They both continued to give me updates for a short while after!

I'll never forget that encounter of evangelism. Not only because it physically and spiritually saved this teenager's life, but because I had no intention of it happening. It reminds me how much God truly loves and cares for His children. Evangelism can happen anywhere, anytime, even when we least expect it!

-Jamie

1

WHAT THE GOSPEL IS

We're often most cautious of the things we're unaware of. A little boy doesn't believe the space underneath his bed is empty. So, he frightens himself with the assumption there's a three eyed monster that makes his home there. Only after his dad confirms there's nothing under the bed does the child feel secure.

I recall the movie *Jack* that came out in the nineties. It was a story of a child named Jack, who was born with a deformity that caused him to grow four times faster than everyone else. By the age of 10, Jack appeared to be 40. The kids his age would walk by his house and tell the story about the "monster" that lived upstairs.

After he convinces his parents to let him, Jack goes to public school. His new classmates are the same children who have been murmuring about him as they walked by his house. It doesn't take long for the children to befriend Jack and get to know his playful character and childlikeness. As they get to know him, they see him as the ten-year-old boy that he is. They become life-long friends.

The things we don't know bring us the most anxiety and suspicion. I have found that many non-believers don't buy into the Gospel story because they haven't heard what it's all about. They're unaware of its truth and the hope that it brings. I only found it fitting to begin this book by revealing the truth about the Gospel. It's vital that we have confidence in what we believe.

First off, every time we believe in the Gospel, we have a fresh revelation of Jesus. It's believing in this Gospel that keeps the fire of God burning inside of us. Second, if we don't know the truth of the Gospel, how can we share it with the broken world? Lastly, what we believe determines how we act. If we don't believe the Gospel, we can't live the Gospel!

I've had many conversations with individuals who don't know the truth about many Christian beliefs. To be effective ambassadors for Christ, we must be firm in our foundation of who He is, what He did and why He did it. The Gospel story is paramount to sharing our faith and showing the world how good our God truly is. This brings me to our first truth about the Gospel - it's good news.

THE GOSPEL IS GOOD NEWS

Everyone loves good news. Good news keeps our lives exciting. It gives us hope for the future and a deep sense of gratitude for our past disappointments. Have you ever received news so exciting that you forgot about everything else in your life for a brief moment? If you answered yes, that's the power of good news.

On the other side of the coin, I haven't met many people that enjoy getting bad news. No one wants to receive an email stating their gym membership rate increased or get a call that their house was destroyed in a fire. Messages like these put dampers on our joy. With the Gospel, no news is bad news. If we aren't sharing the story of Jesus, we are inflicting only bad news on those around us. The Gospel story is the best message we can share. Unlike a house built in one week and burned to the ground the next, the Gospel's goodness never wavers. The story of Jesus will endure in its glory forever.

Even though many reject Jesus, He is still good. His goodness extends to all, not just the church. Non-believers hurt by the church deserve to be told a different narrative of the Gospel. They deserve to know the truth. The redemption they could receive in their lives can't be accessed until they see Jesus as a man of hope and good news. It's not too late to show the broken hearts and souls in our communities that this good news is still relevant to

3

their lives.

King David is my favorite character in scripture. When you read his writings in Psalms, you may conclude that he was an emotional wreck, but what is admirable about David is his constant awareness of God's presence. In one instance, we see him crying out in response to God's goodness:

"I will exalt you, my God the King; I will praise your name for ever and ever. Every day I will praise you and extol your name for ever and ever. Great is the Lord and most worthy of praise; his greatness no one can fathom."

Psalms 145: 1-3

David knew about this wonderful news. He understood the greatness of who Jesus was and gave Him the highest praise for that alone. Jesus is the good news of the Gospel message and nothing can ever take that away. There is no flaw or shortcoming in who Jesus is. This makes the Gospel story the purest message we could ever receive. It should always be on our lips.

All the elements we discuss in this chapter are revelations of this message of good news. Jesus brings reconciliation, restoration, and fresh life to our souls. He made a way for us when there wasn't one. The Gospel story is good; so, we must share it.

THE GOSPEL IS THE PROMISE OF RECONCILIATION FULFILLED

Reconciliation is the restoring back to friendship or harmony between two parties. When there are differences between two people, reconciliation is the process that brings them back together.

From the beginning, God has desired intimacy through reconciliation with us. It's the reason we were created. In Genesis, we see one of the purest and most intimate relationships that history has ever known. When God created Adam, He brought to life the very essence of His deepest desire; to be in relationship with us. He wanted to share Himself with you and me.

As heirs to the fallen world, we can't imagine what this relationship looked like. That's because it was a relationship unlike anything we have ever seen. Adam was focused on God; he could see nothing about himself. God's greatest desire, to be with mankind, was at its peak every time he communed with Adam. In the garden, intimacy was perfect because sin and deceit had yet to enter the world.

Only when we see this picture of intimacy, can we grasp what reconciliation back to the Father looks like. After the fall, the carnal man opened his eyes and noticed himself. Sin entered the heart of man, so God exiled them to the outskirts of the garden. The Gospel story is God's plan to get us back into this relationship with Him. Jesus is our only access to intimacy with the Father.

The Old Testament has several prophecies that allude to the reconciliation between the Father and mankind. These prophecies show us that reconciliation wasn't something that happened by chance. It was a promise that the Father had a plan to fulfill all along. Jeremiah 31:34 says,

"No longer will they teach their neighbor, or say to one another, 'Know the Lord,' because they will all know me, from the least of them to the greatest," declares the Lord. "For I will forgive their wickedness and will remember their sins no more."

Jeremiah 31:34

David also prophesied the new covenant in Psalms 16 when He said,

"Because you will not abandon me to the realm of the dead, nor will you let your faithful one see decay. You make known to me the path of life; you will fill me with joy in your presence, with eternal pleasures at your right hand."

Psalms 16:10-11

Many other prophecies point to the cross and the resurrection of Jesus. Jesus was a very common theme throughout the Old Testament. When we see the Gospel as a promise from God and not just something that happened, we get a better glimpse of His immense love for us. He promised that it would happen. No matter what it took, He would make a way for reconciliation. Even if it cost Him His Son. Knowing He pulled through on this promise gives us a deeper revelation of His love for us. The Gospel story of reconciliation is always good and worthy of sharing.

THE GOSPEL IS THE DISMISSAL OF GOD'S WRATH ON US

Some time ago, I saw a social media post that made me stop and contemplate what Christians believe about God's character. Around the time of this post, California was proposing a bill to ban the sale of Bibles throughout the state. There were several uncontrollable wildfires in California also happening at that time. The post I saw referred to both events. It insinuated that God was pouring out His wrath on California with fires for attempting to ban the sale of Bibles in the state. I cringed at what I read.

To grasp what the Gospel story has done for us, we must know that God's wrath was poured out on Jesus for all of mankind. Those who don't know Jesus will experience the wrath of God on the day of judgement. He is an excellent Father who disciplines His children with love, but He isn't pouring out His wrath on the earth right now:

"For God did not appoint us to suffer wrath but to receive salvation through our Lord Jesus Christ."

1 Thessalonians 5:9

If you have seen Mel Gibson's *Passion of the Christ*, you have witnessed a small glimpse of what God's wrath for us looked like. It's unbearable to visualize the pain that Christ endured on the cross. Every blow and every stripe on His back is a representation of God's wrath for you and I. God's wrath was poured out on His Son so we wouldn't have to endure it.

For those of us who have accepted Jesus as our savior, that wrath is no longer ours to bear. On the day of judgment, God's wrath will pour out on the non-believer. I'm forever grateful for what Jesus endured for me on the cross. The righteousness we have received through our faith in Jesus has dismissed us from God's wrath forever:

"Wealth is worthless in the day of wrath, but righteousness delivers from death."

Proverbs 11:4

Knowing lost souls will one day have to endure the wrath of God motivates me to share the Gospel story. I will discuss more reasons we evangelize later in the book, but this idea is the key motivator for me. I want every lost soul to experience the level of God's mercy I have received through the cross. I praise Jesus for providing a way for me.

It's the desire of my heart to present this message of mercy and grace to the lost.

THE GOSPEL IS THE OPEN DOOR TO OUR RESTORATION

While reconciliation is bringing wholeness back into our relationships with other people, restoration is bringing wholeness within ourselves. One of the biggest lies we can buy into about our self-worth is that we are too far gone to be made holy. For many of us, being spotless is far-fetched, but the blood of Jesus can cover every stain that remains from our past. It doesn't matter where you have been, what you have seen or what you have done, the good news of Jesus takes care of sin once and for all. He has wiped your slate clean. You no longer must live with your old, tattered heart, or corrupt mind! He has restored your soul!

I struggled with writing this book for many reasons. The most daunting fear of mine was not feeling qualified enough. I have no credentials as a writer or evangelist and little experience compared to others, but I'm qualified to write this book because I have a story of restoration that no one else can tell. That's the reason I write, and that's the reason I evangelize. No one can give my account of hope other than me.

My greatest season of restoration took place almost

seven years ago at the age of twenty-three.

My parents split up when I was six, so I grew up despising the word divorce. I made a promise to myself that it would never happen to me. I wanted more success in my marriage than my parents experienced. So, I was heartbroken only a year and a half into my marriage when my wife told me she no longer wanted to be with me. It was shocking. I didn't know what to say or do. I honestly didn't know who I was anymore. I felt like a failure and began battling overwhelming insecurities.

The grace of God pulled heavily on me in this season. I felt the Holy Spirit soften my heart as I became sensitive to His pursuit of me. The Lord placed several people in my life to help me discover who I was in Him again. I remember the night He really grabbed my attention. I went for a drive to pray, listen to some worship music and grab an Oreo blizzard from Dairy Queen. As I sat in the DQ parking lot, I remember being overwhelmed with emotion and longing for an authentic connection with God. I began crying out desperately for a deeper revelation of His love for me.

I didn't even feel God's love for me anymore. I knew in that instant I needed to pursue Him as He was pursuing me. That night I began digging deeper in His Word and spending more time with Him in my secret place. I knew the only way I would feel connected to Him again was to rest in His unconditional, immeasurable love. I knew my heart needed to heal, and I needed to lean into Him for that to happen.

The Lord has done such a significant work in my heart since then. I am renewed through the Gospel, and I'm restored through His immense love for me. I know who He is, and I know who He says I am. That's the promise of restoration that's fulfilled by the Gospel story:

"And the God of all grace, who called you to his eternal glory in Christ, after you have suffered a little while, will himself restore you and make you strong, firm and steadfast. To him be the power for ever and ever. Amen."

1 Peter 5:10-11

God cares less about the lifestyle you have lived or the things from your past that haunt you. You have restoration power living in you because He calls you righteous through the sacrifice of Jesus. He wants to make everything about you whole and complete. He will never fail on His promise to restore you!

THE GOSPEL IS THE ACCESS TO OUR HEAVENLY RIGHTEOUSNESS

I loathe when I am promised something, and I must wait for it. God often has promised me something that didn't come immediately. I know His timing is perfect, but it's still an awful feeling having to wait for something that your heart desperately longs for. Through Jesus, we have a promise of eternity in heaven. The promise of heaven; however, isn't just granted to us on the day we die, it's available now!

When I was younger, I loved eating apples. My grandma used to have a basket she kept full of apples hanging over her kitchen sink. When we were at the grocery store or running an errand, she would promise me an apple when we got home if I behaved while we were out. It worked. Imagine if my grandma had pulled an apple out of her purse while we were sitting at the dentist's office and said, "Here you go, son. You can have this now!" This is what God is offering us. He is holding out His hand saying, "Here's heaven. You can have this now!" Heaven is at our fingertips, but many of us believe it's something we won't experience until we die.

Remember how Jesus taught the disciples to pray? "Your Kingdom come, your will be done, on earth as it is in heaven." (Matthew 6: 9-13) Jesus walked and lived by what He heard the Father saying. He had such a keen ear to the Father's voice because He constantly asked God's will for heaven to be accomplished on earth. Jesus sits next to the Father and intercedes for us in prayer. I can only imagine that He is praying over your life, "On earth as it is in heaven!"

We have a heavenly Father who has already called us His righteousness through our faith in Jesus. There are many heavenly things He wants to bless us with. He wants us to experience heavenly peace, heavenly joy, and even heavenly healing. We have the same access to hear from heaven that Jesus had. "My sheep listen to my voice; I know them, and they follow me." (John 10:27) Through the cross, we have complete access to the Father and His heavenly agenda. Are you okay just settling for heaven one day or do you long to see it invade earth everywhere you go?

Growing up, we used to sing a song, "When we all get to heaven, what a day of rejoicing that will be. When we all see Jesus, we'll sing and shout the victory." There was so much hope in the church building those Sunday mornings as we sang that song. We can all find joy in the promise of heaven. One day we'll see Jesus face to face, and it will be glorious, but why not pray for heaven to invade earth now?

THE GOSPEL IS THE ACCOUNT OF THE HOPE INSIDE OF US

The story of Jesus is so dynamic because it finds and impacts us all in unique ways. It doesn't matter if you have been in church your whole life or if you've just been freed from a dark, unthinkable sin. The unity that comes from

13

the cross joins us all together as the body of Christ. It stirs up hope in our souls for what's coming. People tell me often how they have been transformed by God in a unique way. Every person who has accepted Jesus has their own story of hope that the world desperately needs to hear.

I pray that your salvation story has increased the hope you have, not only for the afterlife, but for the life you live right now. We find hope because we have a promise to spend eternity in heaven. We are also hopeful because we know God has plans for us and He works all things out for the good of those that love Him. It's a hope that can't be taken away because of circumstances; It dwells within us forever. When people notice this hope inside of us, we should always be ready to tell them the good news that we carry. Peter instructs in 1 Peter 3:15,

"But in your hearts revere Christ as Lord. Always be prepared to give an answer to everyone who asks you to give the reason for the hope that you have. But do this with gentleness and respect."

1 Peter 3:15

Our Gospel story is the most powerful weapon we have. When Jesus transforms our lives, He creates this narrative that not only brings hope to us, but it instills hope within others. Revelation 12:11 says that we "overcome by the blood of the lamb and the word of our

14

testimony." That's a powerful promise of hope we get to walk in every day.

Are you ready to give the account of hope inside of you? If someone approached you tomorrow and inquired about your hope, are you confident in what you would say? How has that story transformed your life? We must ask ourselves these questions to have confidence in our personal message of hope. We lack power without it.

When sharing the Gospel, it's important to know the truth about it and how the church is presenting it to non-believers. When we evangelize, we want to do it with excellence. If there's one thing we need to get right, sharing the Gospel is it! Now that we know some truths about what the Gospel is, let's look at a few things we know the Gospel isn't.

2

WHAT THE GOSPEL ISN'T

H ave you ever worked harder on something because you were misinformed about the directions? Maybe your boss placed you in charge of a project and you didn't receive clear objectives. Your teacher may have assigned a paper to write without giving good guidelines to complete it. It's frustrating having to backtrack because you didn't receive good guidance. In the book of Numbers, we see a tragic example of misinformation.

After the Israelites escaped the reign of Pharaoh, they came to the land of Canaan. Canaan was the land God had promised the Israelites they would one day take. The Lord instructed Moses to send twelve spies to observe the land for its harvest and to gauge the strength of its inhabitants. For forty days, the spies kept a close eye on the promised land. At the end of the forty days, the spies returned to report what they saw:

"We went into the land to which you sent us, and it does flow with milk and honey! Here is its fruit. But the people who live there are powerful, and the cities are fortified and very large. We even saw descendants of Anak there. The Amalekites live in the Negev; the Hittites, Jebusites, and Amorites live in the hill country; and the Canaanites live near the sea and along the Jordan." Then Caleb silenced the people before Moses and said, "We should go up and take possession of the land, for we can certainly do it."

Numbers 13: 28-30.

When the spies returned, the Israelites were afraid of the report. Caleb and Joshua were certain they could overcome with the strength of the Lord and take the city. Many others didn't feel as strongly.

Here they were, face to face with the promised land. Instead of taking it, the Israelites wandered in the desert for forty more years because the spies underestimated the promise and strength of the Lord. They believed in the spies' report that rooted itself in fear and disbelief; therefore, they walked away without inheriting the land God had promised. Ironically, Caleb and Joshua were the only two from the Israelite tribe who ever possessed the promised land. The rest eventually perished.

In the first chapter, we discovered some truths about

the Gospel. This chapter is dedicated to exploring areas where Christians have believed bad information concerning it. False misconceptions about the Gospel have plagued Christianity in recent history. Let's keep going to make sure we haven't bought into those misconceptions and prepare ourselves to lead new believers with good information.

THE GOSPEL ISN'T A GET OUT OF HELL FREE CARD

If you died tonight, do you know where you would spend eternity? This is the prompt I have heard so often to entice non-believers to accept Christ. It's the question used most in cold calling, street evangelistic methods. It's a simple decision. When you give someone the option to spend eternity burning in a fire or in heaven, people will choose the latter every time.

The "heaven or hell only" approach has left believers void of valuable realities. When we make the Gospel about entrance into heaven, we leave people longing for the joy Jesus gives in our everyday moments. When the Gospel centers on the afterlife, we deemphasize the relationship with the Father that Jesus died for us to have.

While using hell as a scare tactic often produces quick results, communicating the truth of the Gospel's entirety can be hard. It takes work, patience, and authentic character. If what is being preached invokes fear instead of hope, it isn't the Gospel that's being preached; it's only an agenda to "get people saved."

When I was a kid, I remember going to one of the larger churches in town to watch a drama that was seemingly popular. The play's theme focused on the two destinations of the afterlife: heaven and hell. When the scenes of hell would begin, they would have men dressed as demons with scary masks running into the crowd, grabbing and invoking fear in people. A scare tactic was being used to invite people into giving their life to Christ. Hell is a grave reality, but it's not what the Gospel is about.

This approach has caused believers to treat the Gospel as a "get out of hell free" card. This creates unawareness of the joyous relationship believers can now take part in. When hell is the only thing preached, it's all believers know to measure their righteousness by. If they have escaped hell, they're okay. That's all they were told they needed to do.

When we preach that the Gospel is about hell, we leave people deceived and lost. If eternity is all we talk about when evangelizing, we make death our savior instead of Jesus. The Gospel is about Jesus alone. It's a story that brings us hope and joy, not fear and panic. Only preaching heaven and hell to influence salvation eliminates the relational aspect from the Gospel. Yes, we benefit from a promise with our Father in eternity, but the Gospel isn't a ticket to heaven. We should never underestimate the power of the cross by believing so.

THE GOSPEL IS NOT CHEAP GRACE

There were moments in my adult life where I had to move back home with my parents for a season. Because they were sacrificing their space and privacy for me to stay with them, I wanted to do what I could to help. I would give my dad money and help with things around the house when I could. There may have been days where they felt like I was taking advantage of the situation. I couldn't pay the rent they were asking, and I was having trouble finding a job that would allow me to move out. Despite these things, I wanted to make it a fair deal for them as well. If I had extended my stay because I knew their love and compassion would keep them from asking me to leave, I would have been a participant of cheap grace.

Cheap grace is when we take advantage of someone's kindness and generosity without honoring the price they have paid.

We've all abused the system and taken advantage of the gift of the Gospel. When we sin knowing God will forgive us because that's what He does, we engage in cheap grace. It disheartens me to see this so often within the body of Christ. Many have made it acceptable to live in constant sin without considering the ultimate sacrifice Jesus made for them to be free from it. We have learned to use the cross as a justification of our sins instead of a promise to eradicate them forever.

Cheap grace is when we mooch off our heavenly Father's love for us and receive the gift of His Son without dying to ourselves daily. Because God is so good, He loves us anyway. An authentic revelation of the good news stirs up conviction and a pursuit of holiness within our hearts. The Gospel is a sacred gift we should never take advantage of. Dietrich Bonhoeffer gives a great comparison of cheap grace and costly grace:

"Cheap grace is the preaching of forgiveness without repentance, baptism without discipline, communion without confession, absolution without personal confession. Cheap grace is grace without discipleship, grace without the cross, grace without Jesus Christ, living and incarnate. Costly grace is the treasure hidden in the field; for the sake of it, a man will go and sell all that he has. It is the pearl of great price to buy which the merchant will sell all his goods. It is the kingly rule of Christ, for those who sake a man will pluck out the eye which causes him to stumble; it is the call of Jesus Christ at which the disciple leaves his nets and follows him."

-Dietrich Bonhoeffer.

The enemy has deceived the body into believing we can live without holiness because God has a forgiving nature. We call this way of living "cheap" because the enemy has closed our eyes from seeing everything that forgiveness truly costs. When we have a revelation of the price that Jesus paid, only then will we contemplate the price we'll pay to die to ourselves daily.

THE GOSPEL IS NOT A RELIGIOUS RANKING SYSTEM

Christians are known to be a little snooty at times; not all, but some. Religious and legalistic members of the body of Christ have left little room for interpretation regarding our reputation. We are known for appearing mean, uncaring, and "better" than everyone else. I believe that we are redeeming this reputation, but there are still so many non-believers who have a bad taste for Christian behavior.

Andy Stanley once said that being a Christian doesn't mean we are better than non-believers, we just know that we are better off. The Gospel doesn't create a ranking system or a mindset of comparison. That's what some have made it to be. I have witnessed believers not only acting superior to non-believers, I have also seen them acting better than others who follow Christ. Neither is okay.

Several years ago, a good friend asked me to lead worship for a youth event being held at his house. He also asked a young youth pastor from another church to come preach. I anticipated this opportunity. The small house setting made for an intimate encounter with the teenagers. There were also moments where I was able to add to the conversation. The service, overall, was a powerful encounter with the Lord.

When the event was over, the young pastor told me I had no business giving input during the service. After I asked why, he said because of my lack of credentials as a pastor. He then said when I completed seminary as he had, it would then be acceptable for me to give input. In utter disbelief, I kindly responded and walked off. This isn't new behavior, however. The Pharisees and other religious leaders treated Jesus the same way.

Jesus had a mixed reputation. While there were many who followed Him and obeyed His teachings, there were plenty who had their suspicions. The Jews expected the Messiah to look different from Jesus. They expected a warrior-king; one with great stature and might. They never imagined their savior would be born in a manger of parents with such a low social status. When He began His ministry, the Pharisees, and other religious leaders often questioned Jesus's authority. They looked down on Him and treated Him as a heretic. How shameful it is when we treat others this way.

The love and grace of the Gospel don't leave room for this thought pattern. Jesus's sacrifice on the cross levels the playing field for us all. Our language often represents the idea of "loving your neighbor as yourself," but how we treat people can often tell a different story. We can't be excellent stewards of the heart of the Gospel if we miss the power it has for reconciliation in everyone's life. He loves sinners and saints alike and believe it or not, Jesus died on the cross for others' sins and transgressions just as He died for yours and mine. 2 Corinthians 5:15 reminds us:

"And he died for all, that those who live should no longer live for themselves but for him who died for them and was raised again."

2 Corinthians 5:15

This was a hard concept for the Jews to accept after Jesus had risen from the dead. The Jews were God's people. They were the ones who abided by Mosaic law and found favor in the Lord's sight. I can only imagine how disturbing it must have been for them to hear that outsiders (the Gentiles) were now being allowed into the camp.

Circumcision was a sacred custom of the Jewish culture. The law of Moses put this ritual in place to set the holy apart from the unholy. The Jews took pride in their circumcision and looked down on others who weren't circumcised. In Galatians chapter 5, Paul rebukes this spirit of religion. He implores to the Jews that circumcision is no longer a religious identifier, but "through faith working in love," (Galatians 5:6) they were one with Christ.

Imagine that we as modern-day believers are the Jews, and non-believers are the Gentiles. What does that mean to you? Protestant branches of Christianity no longer circumcise for religious reasons, but today we have filters we often judge other people through. As children of God, it's imperative to look upon others how the Jews now viewed the Gentiles. When the Gentiles surrendered to Him as Lord, He invited them to sit at the table with the rest of the family. The Gospel creates a margin for all to come to the cross and receive God's gift of grace.

Comparing ourselves to non-believers and believers who differ from us doesn't align with the Gospel story. We can't redeem something that we don't care about. If we spend our time comparing, judging and chastising, we can never point people to the heart of Jesus. We will never reach the lost if we believe that we are better than them.

THE GOSPEL IS NOT A REQUEST FOR PAYMENT

One afternoon, my older brother and I were riding through town and he wanted to stop and get a strawberry milkshake from McDonald's. We stopped in, and he offered to buy me one. Chocolate it was! How nice it was for him to offer. The next day, as we were in Wal-Mart, he noticed at the register he only had enough cash for some of his items. Instead of using his card for the rest, he suggested since he bought a milkshake for me the day before, I could buy the items he didn't have enough cash for. Something wasn't right about this at all. I've learned in my life that doing something for someone to get something in return isn't the heart of Jesus at all.

The most humbling aspect of the Gospel is that it's completely free. As believers, we have a natural response to service, but the Lord didn't sacrifice Himself for us to pay Him back. He died on the cross to freely give something to us.

Dwelling on the Gospel is life changing. As we reflect on the events at Calvary, the Father supernaturally injects humility into our character. It's easy to see why our first response to the Lord is praise and thanksgiving. When someone does something kind for you, a response of gratitude is also acceptable. It is also our inclination to believe in our hearts we need to pay that person back. Some of us are serving in our churches or answering the call into ministry to "earn our keep" for what Jesus did on the cross. Jesus didn't give His life for us as a request for payment; He died as the payment that has rendered us debt-free.

Gratitude is the appropriate response to this gift. How we let that response manifest will tell us a lot about how the Gospel story has transformed our lives. Our gratitude toward Jesus often shows up in one of two ways, work or worship.

As I observe the western church, I believe that many of us have allowed our gratitude to motivate a work-based response to the Gospel. We often measure our worth in the Lord by the things we do instead of who we have become. When you look to spiritual disciplines as requirements instead of opportunities for worship, a response of work sets in. The Gospel doesn't give us a reason to work; it gives us a reason to rest. We no longer must fight the tension between sin and holiness. Our salvation is no longer something we must work for.

Worship is the response that brings pleasure to our Father. Scripture says He is enthroned upon the praises of His people, not their works. Worship is how we give God the honor and adoration He deserves. In my eBook *Going Deeper in Worship*, I talk about some practical things that will increase our intimacy with the Father as we approach Him in worship. We should make it a daily discipline to learn how to worship the Father well. Telling the Lord how good He is should be our first response to the cross. Everything else is a by-product of our worship to Him.

Everything we do should give God honor and glory. It's okay to serve in your church, read your Bible, and sing on the worship team. Those are beautiful things. When we practice these acts of service to the Lord with an intent to pay Him back, we aren't bringing glory to Him through worship; we are attempting to glorify ourselves through our works. Worship proclaims, "God, You are so good!" while work says, "God, this is how good I have to be."

Understanding the different perspectives of worship and work will help us behold the beauty of the Gospel. If we measure ourselves by our works, we take on the belief that we will never be good enough to hit the mark. Our response in worship partners with the truth that through the Gospel, we are more than good enough. We don't have to work to fill in the gap that Jesus paid for with His blood. Authentic works come from a genuine response in worship.

THE GOSPEL IS NOT A MEANS TO AN END

In our attempts to evangelize, it's easy to turn the Gospel story into an agenda. The Holy Spirit often reminds me that the Gospel isn't about trying to persuade someone into a decision. We want people to follow Jesus, but sharing the Gospel isn't about their decision. The centrality of the Gospel is about our unconditional love for the lost; no matter how they respond.

29

I have a friend Carlos, who I love dearly. We've been friends since middle school and became closer during our tenth-grade year. Carlos experienced hurt from the church at a very early age. I've shared the Gospel with him frequently. He once told me it was refreshing for him to see someone who loved Jesus the way I do. He said he has never seen a genuine faith like that before.

While that's an honoring compliment, it helped me realize that sharing the Gospel with Carlos wasn't contingent upon his decision. The only agenda in sharing the Gospel is showing him God's love. I can't imagine what I would do to his impression of Jesus if I stopped loving him because he didn't accept the Gospel message. If I rejected our friendship because of his decision, I could deter him from ever being open to talking about God again.

In our post-Christian culture, evangelism is more effective when it's centered on relationships. People respond with receptivity when the Gospel story becomes a conversation instead of a presentation. Treating others the way Jesus did draws them closer to the Father than our own manufactured agendas. It seems basic, but it's often the thing we misconstrue the most.

As we approach the practicalities of evangelism, Let's remember we are now in constant communication with a generation that craves authentic relationships. Genuine conversations can help begin the healing process that must take place, especially with those who have a bad history with Christianity. We must backtrack in the areas where the church of the past has left distaste for God. The millennial generation and Generation Z are excellent at sniffing out phony agendas. If they feel you have one, your voice will become irrelevant. We must treat the Gospel as the love story it is and not the means to an end we've often made it to be.

Now that we have clarity on the truth of the Gospel, let's look at why we share it and reasons we often don't. In these next two chapters, I hope you regain the confidence you may be lacking. I know you will become a Christian on a mission to win lost souls for the Kingdom!

PRAYER FOR HEALING AT THE GYM

One day, a close friend and I went to the gym to work out and love on people. As we walked through the gym, I shared, "Jesus loves you, so much" to the people we were passing by. As we were working out, I noticed a woman with a cast on and immediately said to my friend, "Oh look! She has a cast. Let's go pray with her." Without hesitation, we went over to the woman who also had her mom with her.

As we were walking over to them, I felt fear try to come over me. I felt physically cold. I live a lifestyle of evangelism, which, as biblical Christians, we're called to do in alignment with the great commission. I rarely experience fear because I know it's a lie from the devil and I take it captive to the truths of what Jesus says about me. God says I haven't been given a spirit of fear but of power, love and a sound mind. Scripture also says I am a partaker of the divine nature of God, and there is no fear in Him; therefore, as I experienced this, I knew the devil hated what we were doing. This fear was not my fear, but the devils. The devil is terrified of believers who walk like Jesus and share His love to the world!

The two ladies were really kind to us. The fear that tried to overtake me was invalid. I said as I approached them, "Hey, how's it going?" I followed with, "Jesus loves you so much, and your lives are really important." They responded with gratitude and I said, "I noticed you're wearing a brace," and asked if I could pray for her arm. "God doesn't like for you to have a hurt wrist and He wants to heal it right now," I continued.

The mom of the woman said, "I was just praying for her healing this morning because this is disrupting her career. She does professional body building." She also said that this was an answer to her prayer; that we showed up on the same day she was praying. So, we prayed. I also blessed them in other ways during the prayer, and we released the Kingdom of heaven right there in the gym. She wasn't willing to remove the cast to test it out, so we didn't see if God healed her in that moment or not.

As I was praying, I received a word of knowledge for the woman about her ability to sing. I revealed the word of knowledge I received. She said she used to sing, but she had been having difficulty with her voice for a while, causing it to hurt and sound rough. I told her, "God will heal that too!" We prayed, and after the prayer, her voice still sounded raspy. But I encouraged her I would remain in prayer for her and that I still believed God would heal her voice. We left and were all encouraged and filled with hope!

-Drew

3

WHY WE SHARE THE GOSPEL

We all enjoy celebrating those we love. The community I call family is excellent at championing each other's successes. We often get together to celebrate engagements, gender reveals, or graduations. It's beautiful when we can share the important things happening in our lives with each other.

Just as we discussed in chapter one, sharing and receiving good news is fun and exciting. It's one thing that we're all good at. When's the last time you received good news and didn't tell anyone? It's simple. It's a natural behavior for us to talk about positive things.

The Gospel is no different. The word Gospel means good news. I'll argue that it's the best message you could possibly tell someone. Just like the big announcements we celebrate, the Gospel brings joy and hope to each of our lives. It's a message of transformation and healing. We share it because of our instinct to share good news.

Sharing this message of hope is more crucial now, in our post-Christian culture, than it's ever been in our country's past. Post-Christian is a term used to describe Christianity as it pertains to current society. We were once known as a predominantly Christian nation. We can no longer make such a claim. Christians, for the first time, make up less than 50 percent of America's population. I encourage you to look up some research regarding Christianity in America administered by the Barna Group. These numbers will make it clear why it's urgent we step into our evangelistic callings.

As we move through the rest of the book, let's keep this post-Christian ideology at the forefront of our minds. According to the numbers, more than half the people you meet today don't believe in Jesus. That's a lot of opportunity for you to share the Gospel message with someone! The moments to evangelize are everywhere, and we carry the ultimate message of hope!

If you need more motivation than that, let's continue. We will go over more reasons to evangelize throughout this chapter, beginning with one of the more obvious reasons; we have been commanded to do so.

WE HAVE BEEN COMMANDED TO DO SO

In Mark 16:15, Jesus tells His disciples, "Go into all the world and preach the Gospel to all creation." These are His first words recorded in the book of Mark after the resurrection. This was the most important command He instructed the disciples to follow after He rose from the grave.

With this command comes our response to obey. In 1 John 5:2-3, we are told, "This is how we know that we love the children of God: by loving God and carrying out His commands. In fact, this is love for God: to keep His commands. And His commands are not burdensome." Our obedience shows our love for the Lord. Sharing the good news with others is an overflow of God's love to the world through us. We reciprocate that love back to Him when we obey the command to tell the world of His goodness.

We must remember, the Lord commanded us to evangelize because it's important to Him. It's often our first inclination to evangelize out of obedience or to avoid guilt, but we should obey this command to honor the importance it carries to the Lord. When we evangelize to bring joy to His heart, we can turn that avoidance of guilt into compassion for the lost.

Believe it or not, there are Christians who don't take the command to evangelize very seriously. Some would rather tolerate other's beliefs and ideas; they think it's more beneficial to avoid offending. I urge you to obey this command with the utmost importance. We weren't given the gift of the Holy Spirit to be passive in sharing the Gospel. We should be respectful of others' ideas and beliefs, but we shouldn't let that stop us from spreading the love of Jesus to the lost. This is a crucial command to obey. I pray that you will honor it rightly.

THE KINGDOM IS AT HAND

I've watched basketball my entire life; It's one of my favorite sports. It's a fast-paced game and it can be very intense. The first half is usually interesting for serious fans, but for your average basketball watcher, the good stuff doesn't happen until the end. As the clock winds down, urgency arises and both teams sense the outcome of the game hanging in the balance. Players feel the pressure to make big plays, and every second becomes more valuable than the last.

In Matthew 3:2, John the Baptist prepares the way for Jesus by instructing the people to repent for the Kingdom is at hand. In basketball terms, he is saying, "Get your act together! It's the end of the 4th quarter and the game is on the line!"

Unfortunately, some of us share our faith like it's still the first quarter. We act like we have an abundance of time to tell the lost about Jesus. Scripture tells us the day of the

Lord will come like a thief in the night. We may be nonchalant about sharing our faith now, but we are losing precious time. You may be waiting for the right time to talk to a friend or loved one about Jesus. The right time is now. The clock could run out before you know it. We should have urgency in sharing the Gospel.

Being urgent doesn't mean we frantically share the Gospel without prayer or tact. Having urgency means we are always on high alert for opportunities to share our faith. It also means we set aside certain moments in our day to talk to specific people about Jesus. We must be ready to share the Gospel like the game is on the line!

PEOPLE NEED JESUS NOW

As explored earlier, we often relegate our salvation message to a "heaven or hell only" ideology. By doing this, we fail to address the reality that people need Jesus now. By focusing on the afterlife as an approach to "get people saved," we have devalued the Gospel's role in bringing instant transformation to the new believer. We have stymied the relational aspect of the Gospel story.

I've heard people say they will focus on their faith later in life. It's almost as if believing in Jesus is too much of a burden. There are many reasons people put a relationship with Jesus off, but it's often rooted in the idea that salvation is for the afterlife. Some people believe if they "get right" with God before they die, they'll be okay.

When we see the Gospel story as hope for our future instead of security for our eternity, we see the beauty of the Gospel message to heal our broken souls. It's no hidden secret that depression rates are at an all-time high. Other factors like suicide, anxiety, and divorce have also increased over recent years. Even among believers, it's evident some are lacking a foundation that allows them to believe in the Gospel's beauty. Now, more than ever, we need the saving grace of the Gospel.

As believers, we know that people who don't follow Jesus have voids in their lives. They lack hope for their present circumstances and futures. The lost and their spiritual needs should always compel us with compassion to speak with them about Jesus. He's the One who can fill those voids and bring hope and peace to their situations. The lost desperately need Him and we carry that message of hope. There should always be a heavy desire to share the Gospel now instead of later.

Reflect on the people you know who need Jesus. Through a Christlike lens that recognizes brokenness and hurt, we can see how badly the lost need salvation. We can't assume those who need Him will eventually have a revelation of Him. We also can't put it off on someone else to share the Gospel with them later. As we share the good news of hope with the lost, they can respond to receive restoration in their greatest time of need, which is now.

NON-BELIEVERS ARE GENUINELY
UNINFORMED

Some concepts in the first two chapters may have challenged how you view the Gospel. As we grow in our Christian walk, we develop fresh perspectives and can sometimes lose sight of foundational truths. That's common. That's why we constantly come back to the Gospel's simplicity; so we don't dilute it with faulty concepts.

If you were freshly exposed to the Gospel, imagine how revealing its truth must be to non-believers who are uninformed about the Gospel. It will change their lives forever!

It's one thing for non-believers to reject Christ for who He is, it's another for them to reject a version of Christ that isn't true. As believers, it's our responsibility to make sure the lost are told the truth of the Gospel. I believe as we expose the truth to those who are uninformed, they will believe and surrender to Jesus. Scripture tells us it's the truth that sets us free. (John 8:31-32) Many lost souls are wandering in the wilderness because they have been misinformed and are unaware of the truth.

I have gone through cycles of weight loss during my lifetime. Losing weight and gaining weight are things I am consistent with. One day at the gym, I was lifting weights and a man approached me to ask me about my workout routine. He'd seen me in the gym for several weeks and was curious about my process. This guy was very lean and muscular. In our conversation, he gave me some pointers on weight loss and muscle gain. He even exposed things about the human anatomy I was misinformed about. Because of his stature and how he talked with confidence, I was persuaded to change some things about my weight loss and muscle gain routine.

When we are exposed to the truth, we can make better decisions. This applies to non-believers as well. When they hear the truth of the Gospel, they can make their decision based on that truth instead of their faulty misconceptions.

Discovering where the lost are misinformed will be a by-product of asking good questions. In our efforts to understand people's perspectives, we can identify the flaws in what others think and use solid theology to point them to the truth of Jesus. With help from the Holy Spirit and the Christlikeness we obtain through our salvation, we can successfully point them to the realities of the Gospel.

OUR LOVE AND COMPASSION COMPELS US

In Matthew chapter 20, there's a story where Jesus is walking from one town to another. As He is making His way through the crowd, two blind men shout to Him and inquire about receiving sight in their eyes. Verse 34 says. "Jesus had compassion on them and touched their eyes.

Immediately they received their sight and followed him."

Compassion touched the heart of the Lord, so He extended healing and restoration to the hurting. Our empathy towards the broken and hurting should compel us to share the hope of Jesus with them. So often, we want to evangelize because we feel it's a requirement. Treating evangelism as a religious duty instead of an opportunity to love people stunts our compassion for the lost.

Some Christians don't share the Gospel because they lack compassion. I used to blame not evangelizing on my introverted character; I was too shy. The truth is, I didn't care. Compassion will override every excuse for not sharing the Gospel. I know other factors keep us from evangelizing, (more of that in the next chapter) but when compassion compels us to share, we will find a way to share.

WE HAVE THE ANSWER. WHY NOT?

My family has been affected by a fatal respiratory disease, Cystic Fibrosis (CF). It's a genetic lung disease that takes the lives of many young individuals at an early age. I follow the advancements and research for CF, but no cure yet exists. Imagine how cruel it would be for someone to discover the cure for a disease like CF and not share it. It's selfish for us to claim that we have the answer of hope for the lost and keep it all to ourselves.

I am enamored by the response the apostles had to their encounter with the risen Jesus. After they saw Him, they knew they carried the answer the rest of the world would need. With urgency, they traveled all over the Middle East to proclaim this powerful message of hope. Not only did they tell others about Jesus, they also made it their life mission. Jesus was so essential to their lives, they were willing to die to tell the world about Him, and most of them did.

What does it mean to know you have the answer to everyone's despair? We may think we are doing others a favor by not forcing our faith on them, but that's not true. The lost world needs people like you and me to share the Gospel with them. Some don't even know there's a problem until we show them the answer.

One morning, I was reading in a local coffee shop and struck up a conversation with a woman writing a paper for school. She mentioned she was working on a geology assignment and we got into a gripping conversation about the creation of the earth. As we talked, she discussed the big bang theory, and I was able to tell her about my belief in God. She said the class she was taking led her to ponder what she believed and that my account of God as creator was another idea she'd been exploring. I didn't lead her to the Lord that day, but in a God-ordained moment, I was able to provide some answers about God this woman had been searching for.

44

YOUR STORY IS UNIQUE

Windshields on a car are thick. One of my favorite movies is a low budget film called *Short Term 12*. There's a scene in the movie where the leader of an orphanage and one of its teenagers smash in a windshield with a wooden baseball bat. As they strike the windshield, you can see the windshield slowly cracking and shattering. Eventually, with enough force and one final blow, the windshield finally gives way and the bat makes it through to the other side. You never know when your testimony will be that final blow that causes someone to surrender their life to the Lord!

We all have unique stories. While there are people who respond with receptivity to my testimony, others need someone like you! How many people shared Jesus with you before you believed? There came a moment when you heard the story of Jesus and it finally clicked. As you attempt to share the Gospel, you will find that many people who accept Jesus have already heard what you are telling them, they just needed to hear your unique story for it to click!

Christians telling their testimony has been the number one vehicle for evangelism for the past 2000 years. By the blood of the Lamb and the word of our testimony, we've been given the tools we need to continue being successful at evangelism. You have a unique story. There are lost souls who need to hear how the Lord has transformed your heart.

Evangelism hasn't always been natural, but when I learned that I could reach the lost by telling my story, I found joy in letting people into my broken and redeemed places. I'll let you in as well!

I grew up with two older brothers. They were both born with the genetic lung disease, Cystic Fibrosis that I mentioned earlier. They were in and out of hospitals and limited with the things they could physically do. Individuals with Cystic Fibrosis have brief life spans. At the writing of this book, the average age a CF patient lives to be is 37 years old. When I was a child, that number was in the mid-twenties.

My oldest brother passed away when he was nineteen, and my other brother passed away five years later, at twenty-one. Each death stung a little differently for me, but none-the-less, they hurt.

There were many questions I battled the Lord with, even at such a young age. One question I learned to ask was, "What now?" I knew early in my grieving process that God would do powerful things through the restoration He was doing within me. I knew at 16 years old I would be a youth pastor. I longed to minister to teenagers experiencing the same hurts that I had.

I look at close members in my family who still feel the sting of my brothers' deaths. That sting is no longer there for me. Because Jesus freed me from that hurt, I can use my story to bring restoration in others' lives who are battling the same emotions. This is just one layer of my story that God has used to allow me to share the Gospel. He took the lowest place in my life and gave me a unique story to share with the world. He has done the same for you!

I love sharing the Gospel because my story and purpose are both uniquely formed by the Lord. I encourage you to look at your moments of healing and ask God how He can use them in bringing the lost back to Him. He has given you a story just as unique. It's time for people to hear about the hope that dwells inside of you. Your story may shatter the windshield of someone's heart and reveal to them the goodness of the Gospel. I urge you to share it!

We have numerous reasons to evangelize, although many still find reasons not to. In the next chapter, I want to explore these reasons and debunk the myths of evangelism that keep us from sharing the Gospel. As we go through this next chapter, I pray you discover some reasons you don't share the Gospel as well. My goal is to shed light on the areas that will empower you to share the good news no matter what!

4

REASONS WE DON'T SHARE
THE GOSPEL

I t's no surprise. Christians haven't been very active in sharing their faith lately. When was the last time someone you didn't know started a conversation with you about Jesus? It's been a while for me. Chances are, if believers were urgent in sharing the Gospel message, someone would evangelize to you at some point too.

There are battles we fight with the enemy that prevent us from sharing the Gospel. As we begin this chapter, I encourage you to reflect on fears and insecurities you may have in sharing your faith. As you discover your own reasons, I know you will overcome them by gaining confidence in your abilities to evangelize.

Several weeks ago, I posted a question on Facebook for people to discuss reasons they don't share their faith. I want to share a couple of those reasons with you throughout this chapter. These are genuine answers from people just like you and me. I hope you can glean from them as I have.

FEAR OF REJECTION

The fear of rejection has crippled me my entire life. I have struggled with insecurities and the thoughts that I may not be good enough. Rejection carves a gaping hole into who we are as people. It crushes our identity and causes us to question our worth. No one enjoys being rejected.

Facebook Post: "What are some fears you have in sharing your faith with others?"

Facebook user one said this:

"I'm scared of people attaching a stigma to me and putting me in a box. I feel like people immediately assume I think they are doing wrong when I am a super non-judgmental person. I just want to talk to them about God's love."

What this user expressed was the fear of rejection. It isn't total rejection, but it's a fear that someone won't see their true intentions. When non-believers have narrow views of Christianity and put our faith in a religious box, they are rejecting a vital part of our identity. Our faith in the Lord has shaped who we are. If people fail to see our

Christlike love for them, we take that rejection personally.

Our commission to evangelize is exhilarating. The possibility of introducing the lost to Jesus compels us to shout the Gospel message from the rooftops! It's when fear creeps in that we take a back seat and let our comfort zones dictate what we do. We often ponder how evangelistic conversations could go badly and decide the risk isn't worth the reward. When we do this, we selfishly attach our identity and self-worth to the outcome. This causes us to avoid evangelistic opportunities because we know rejection will shatter how we see ourselves.

Jesus knew our flesh could make evangelism about us. If we fear rejection while sharing our faith, we have made the Gospel message more about ourselves than we've made it about Him. In Luke 10:16, Jesus tells us, "Whoever listens to you listens to me; whoever rejects you rejects me; but whoever rejects me rejects him who sent me." This verbal declaration should empower us to share the Gospel without fear of rejection. When the lost reject our message, they're rejecting Jesus, not us. This revelation will obliterate this fear and compel us to share the Gospel with everyone we interact with. If we believe the Gospel points to Jesus and not us, we free ourselves from rejection and share the Gospel freely.

WE FEEL INSUFFICIENT IN KNOWLEDGE

It's terrifying when someone asks a question you don't have the answer to, especially a subject as sacred as the Gospel. Movies portray this fear often. A teacher stands in front of the class and calls out the boy who is sleeping to answer a question. He raises his head frantically and feels humiliated because he is unaware of the subject they are discussing.

It can humiliate us when we don't have answers about our faith. We often feel unqualified due to a lack of knowledge. For this reason, many don't share the Gospel. We sometimes feel we will do more harm than good if we can't articulate an answer to a question correctly. It's admirable to want to represent Christ well; however, we must know it's not our intellect that draws people to Jesus.

In John chapter 9, there's a story of a blind man. In his home city, they knew him as the blind beggar. The others didn't associate with him or consider him to be an essential contributor to society. As Jesus walks by, He notices this man and instantly heals his sight. This healing causes a big uproar in the city. They take it before the religious leaders for investigation. As they interrogate the (once) blind man, all he knew to tell was his experience. After an exhausting dialogue between the religious leaders and the blind man, they ask him one final time, who the man was that healed him. His response should encourage us as sharers of the faith:

25; "Whether he is a sinner or not, I don't know. One thing I do know. I was blind but now I see!" 30-33; The man answered, "Now that is remarkable! You don't know where he comes from, yet he opened my eyes. We know that God does not listen to sinners. He listens to the godly person who does his will. Nobody has ever heard of opening the eyes of a man born blind. If this man were not from God, he could do nothing."

John 9: 25; 30-33

This man knew nothing about Jesus. Faced with persecution, he declared He must be from God because of the healing he experienced through Him. He lacked knowledge and intellect, but his encounter with the Lord enabled him to share the good news. Just the same, it's our experiences with the Lord that draw the lost to Him, not the information we know.

We aren't expected to know everything about scripture. Studying God's Word is a vital aspect of our faith, but our knowledge isn't what leverages our efforts in evangelism. Our ability to communicate the Gospel gains power as we share the areas the Lord has transformed in our lives. By sharing our testimonies, we draw people to our humility and relentless faith. The lost will find more value in our experiences with Jesus than they will in our intellectual conversations.

But what about the questions we're asked and don't

have the answers to?

Recently, I was talking with a group of friends at work and the subject of religion came up. They all know where I stand in my faith, and someone asked me a question that genuinely stumped me. "Where do dinosaurs fit into the timeline of creation?"

Of all the things I could get stumped on, I never thought it would be dinosaurs. I said, "I don't know." Because they knew my heart was genuine and they've heard my testimonies of transformation, it wasn't a big deal to them I didn't know the answer.

People will ask us questions we don't have the answers to. Even with extravagant reading and studying, we'll never have every answer. That can be intimidating if we think our knowledge entices non-believers to accept Jesus. It's foolish to think salvation rides on what we know.

Instead, we should remember Luke 12:11-12, "When you are brought before synagogues, rulers and authorities, do not worry about how you will defend yourselves or what you will say, for the Holy Spirit will teach you at that time what you should say." This promise released the apostles from persecution frequently as they responded to religious leaders with the guidance of the Holy Spirit. As we lean into the Spirit, He will always give us the words to say.

We place pressure on ourselves by expecting our

knowledge to determine the outcome. A decision to follow Christ is a combination of the authentic love we present and what the Holy Spirit has already been doing. When we rely on the Holy Spirit to guide our words, we partner with the Father in communicating what that person needs to hear. We may feel insufficient in knowledge, but that gives us the opportunity to lean into the Spirit and allow Him to do the transformative work.

LACK OF EMPATHY

Since you are reading a book on evangelism, I have faith you want to reach the lost for Jesus. In knowing this book focuses on others finding salvation, the first step you took in picking it up was a selfless one; however, there are some that have no desire to read about evangelism because of its focus on other people.

We lack general empathy for others when we focus too much on ourselves. Our faith in Jesus should be rooted in surrender to Him and sacrifice to others. So often, our faith asks, "What can Jesus do for me?" Instead, we should ask, "What can I do for Him?" If we take the focus of our faith off ourselves and place it upon Him, it creates space in our hearts to obtain compassion and empathy for the lost.

Authentic empathy originates as we let the heart of God become one with ours. Our compassion for others is a direct response to the humility of the Gospel in our lives. If you find you lack compassion towards the lost, I encourage you to fast and pray for God to shift this area of your heart. You can live your entire life as an evangelist, but without love for the lost, all you are is a clanging cymbal (1 Corinthians 13:1).

WE WOULD RATHER KEEP THE PEACE

Facebook user two said this in response to my post:

"In short, my fear has stemmed from the possibility of ruining relationships."

The fear of destroying our relationships is a monster of its own; It's tricky to navigate. There's a tension between sharing the Gospel and poking the bear. Even though we desperately want our friends to know Jesus, we often fear the relationship may not be the same if the conversation goes badly. It's risky talking about Jesus with our lost friends. If the risk seems too big, we may avoid talking about Him altogether.

Earlier, we discussed that the Gospel wasn't a means-to-an-end. Our relationships should never be based solely on our desire to evangelize. Instead, through our intimate and trustworthy relationships, we can love our friends and share the Gospel without fear of rejection. A friend's decision, or lack thereof, should never be a reason for us to abandon the relationship. When we show we love them more than their decision, we reveal the unconditional love of God. This draws them closer to Jesus than our means-to-an-end agendas do.

We have 80-100 years of life to form meaningful relationships. What are those relationships worth on the other side if we aren't telling people about Jesus? Can we consider ourselves real friends if we're worried about losing their friendship over their salvation? By sharing the Gospel with them, we maximize potential to give those temporary relationships eternal value.

I was nervous to talk with Ben about Jesus. One evening, on my way to pick him up, I felt the Lord pulling on my heart to share the Gospel with him. When he got in the car, I was listening to a worship radio station. He turned the volume up as we rode and said he liked the vibe of the song. He knew it was a Christian song and asked me what it was talking about.

We talked for a few minutes about the song and what it meant. I told him before he got in the car, I felt the Lord asking me to speak with him about salvation. I asked him some questions about his background and where he stood on Christianity. I didn't want to push anything on him, but I felt the Lord using that conversation to speak to him. As I answered some questions he had and shared some truths about the Gospel, I saw the Lord softening his heart. After our conversation, he thanked me for speaking to him about Jesus. No one had ever done that before.

Benjamin didn't receive Christ that day, but I planted a seed. We remain excellent friends, today. He knows that my love for him is genuine. We talk about God occasionally, and he asks me questions from time to time. Because we built our friendship on compassion and trust, he knows that I love him even though we don't share the same beliefs.

You don't always have to choose between sharing the Gospel and losing a friendship. An authentic relationship allows us to share the Gospel without fear we will destroy it.

Sharing the Gospel will always leave an impression of Jesus on someone's heart. They may draw closer to you, or they may pull away, but risking your friendships to introduce the lost to Jesus is rewarding. When we are obedient and plant seeds, they can take root and birth a transformational response to the Gospel. It's more rewarding when our grace and compassion allow us to maintain our friendships through the process!

WE HAVEN'T HAD A REVELATION OF THE RISEN JESUS

In Mark chapter 3, Jesus is making His way through the crowds, proclaiming He is the healer of the sick and forgiveness of sins. What a bold statement! He was healing, forgiving, and people were gathering. As He is speaking to the crowds in His hometown, His family (including His brother James) comes out into the streets to get Him. They insist to those gathered that He is "out of His mind." That must have been an enormous blow. Have you ever had a close family member turn their back on you or publicly shame you? The people that know us best are the ones we expect to stand up for us the most. Jesus' family let Him down.

It's clear, in his New Testament book, that James was no longer a skeptic of who his brother was. From denouncing Him in the streets to giving his life for the Gospel, something changed, but what? James had an encounter with the risen savior (1 Corinthians 15:7) and it redirected the course of his life forever.

Just like many apostles, James lived a martyr's life. He died to tell others about the Gospel. Whenever we see someone encounter the resurrected Jesus, we see disbelief turn to faith and skepticism turn to servanthood. The apostles lived radical lives once they saw Jesus raised from the dead.

I believe there are post-Christian followers that have yet to experience the risen savior. Many of our encounters with Jesus stop at the cross. We can often be like James and many others before they laid their eyes upon Jesus as the resurrected Messiah; lethargic and somewhat skeptical because we haven't yet realized we've been raised with Him. When we see Jesus as our resurrected savior, I believe a desire to share the Gospel with the world will explode from within us.

I remember the nights I would lay awake and reflect on my sins. I prayed and asked forgiveness as I went down my list. Every time I messed up, I went back to the cross and asked for forgiveness all over again. I was still operating under the old covenant. The cross was as far as my salvation went. My life didn't resemble what it looked like to be raised with Christ.

Scripture tells us that Jesus wiped away our sinful nature for good. We now walk in the revelation of the empty grave and have confidence in knowing we've been set free from the bondage of sin. God looks at us with the same eyes He sees Jesus through; this includes seeing us as His righteousness. When we see Christ as a resurrected savior, we fully grasp the victory and joy we've been freed to operate in. This revelation makes it difficult to keep quiet about our faith!

The resurrection affirmed the apostles' belief in Jesus, but it was Pentecost that gave them boldness and power to share the Gospel fearlessly. We should never try to evangelize without the power of the Holy Spirit. In the next chapter, we will discuss some truths about the Holy Spirit, debunk myths that the church carries about Him, and explore how He helps in our efforts to share the Gospel.

THE SOBERING LOVE OF JESUS

Once, when I was involved with my church's youth ministry, we went out to witness and tell others about Jesus. We split up into groups of three and began speaking to people as we felt led by the Lord. A friend and I felt led to pray for this man who was drunk at the time. We were a little on edge but felt led to share about the love of Jesus. As we shared the Gospel and prayed with him, the man supernaturally sobered up. He looked confused at first but started crying because he could feel the presence of the Lord. He believed he had done too much in his past to be loved and forgiven by God! He said, "I can't believe He would love me like that." We then loved on Him and shared about the unconditional love of Jesus! Wow! There is definitely power in what Jesus died to purchase for us. Hallelujah!

*   -Presley*

5

EVANGELIZING WITH THE HOLY SPIRIT

When telling someone about Jesus, I rarely ask them to say a prayer of salvation. Over my lifetime, I've seen many evangelists relegate salvation to what we call the "sinner's prayer." We must believe there's something bigger happening in our conversations with the lost. Honest surrender to the Lord produces transformation from within, not just a confession from the mouth. While it's a powerful experience to lead someone in a prayer of salvation, here are the reasons I don't make it my priority.

First, "the prayer" isn't the agenda. Starting conversations to invite someone into a prayer is a by-product of the wrong motive. Evangelism only has one agenda; to love. People are good at discerning false motives in their conversations, and they have seen phony agendas in evangelism before. Many non-believers are skeptical of evangelistic conversations and will flee at the first notion of an inauthentic agenda. Genuine love will be the only agenda that captivates the heart of the non-believer. A preconceived effort to get to a prayer stunts the invitation for the Spirit to have His way.

Second, "the prayer" doesn't solidify someone's salvation. As discussed earlier, many Christians have falsely believed that a prayer keeps them from hell. Romans 10:9 states that, "If you declare with your mouth, "Jesus is Lord," and believe in your heart that God raised Him from the dead, THEN you will be saved." Believing in our hearts the work of Jesus for our lives is the cornerstone of our salvation. If we approach evangelism with a prayer as an end goal, we may lead someone to confess with their mouths, but not emphasize how the condition of their heart plays a role in their salvation.

Last, I can't save anyone. Sharing the Gospel is a joyous role that I get to be a part of in introducing someone to Jesus, but the Holy Spirit does the work of drawing the lost to the Father. John 16:8 explains to us it's the Holy Spirit that convicts the world of its sin, not us. By making the prayer the agenda, we are placing the weight of our evangelistic efforts on our own shoulders. The pressure we tend to put on ourselves to lead someone into a prayer of salvation comes from the belief that it's our persuasion that causes someone to decide. Allowing the Spirit to operate in our evangelistic conversations takes the pressure off us to "perform." An agenda of love will have the largest impact in sharing the Gospel. You may not lead someone in the prayer of salvation, but you may plant a seed that will make them receptive to the next person who shares the Gospel with them.

When we set this prayer agenda aside, we make room for the Holy Spirit. His involvement is the ingredient that shifts evangelism from a dead work to one that speaks life and transformation. Jesus explains to the disciples that He must ascend so He could send the Holy Spirit as our helper. He said it would be better for us to have the Spirit than to have Him. Evangelizing without the guidance of the Holy Spirit is impossible. We leave so much up to chance when we try to share the Gospel on our own. Let's explore more about this helper and why He is vital in our efforts to share Christ with the world!

THE UPPER ROOM

In Acts chapter 2, we see the greatest outpouring of love known to man. After the Lord promised He would send the Holy Spirit, He instructed the disciples not to leave town until He arrived. 120 faithful believers gathered in a room, waiting for this promise from the Lord. These people didn't know exactly what they were waiting for, but they were patient; and just like that, it happened:

"Suddenly a sound like the blowing of a violent wind came from heaven and filled the entire house where they were sitting. They saw what seemed to be tongues of fire that separated and came to rest on each of them. All of them were filled with the Holy Spirit and began to speak in other tongues as the Spirit enabled them."

Acts 2:2-4

This passage is preached from charismatic pulpits on Pentecost Sunday, usually with an emphasis on speaking in tongues. Before you checkout, I understand there are differing views on this idea of speaking in tongues in the modern church. I will discuss that later in this chapter, hoping to put into perspective why many of us feel the way we do about it. The gift of tongues is powerful, but the filling of the Holy Spirit is far greater. I believe when we agree on this truth, it makes the subject of tongues less tense and offensive.

I asked the Lord for a vision as I desired to see a deeper meaning behind the events of the upper room. When there is an idea or concept too expansive to comprehend, I enjoy asking for pictures or visions that will help me understand it. Before I expound upon the vision, I'll ask you to think about the barrier that separated us from an intimate relationship with God. Imagine an unclimbable wall that prevented us from reaching the Father; there's no way over and no way around. Because of this wall, it was impossible to be in perfect relationship with Him. This isn't how God originally designed it to be.

When I asked God for this vision of the upper room, He showed me this enormous wall that separated us. On the side across from where I stood, I saw Him pushing mightily. He was trying to reach me, but the wall was too stout. As He pushed, a dove swooped down and came crashing through the wall, allowing the love of God to overwhelm me.

The Holy Spirit came crashing down into the upper room to lavish the 120 with His uncontrollable love! This was the first moment without separation between the Father and mankind since the fall of Adam. The death, burial, and resurrection made a way for that wall to be destroyed, but the Holy Spirit was the fulfillment of God's promise to be intimate with us again! We can't see the gift of the Holy Spirit without knowing He is the manifestation of God's love given to His children!

This gift of love is essential in our efforts to evangelize. Without it, we are powerless. This love from the Father should be a constant flow of grace and mercy, with no restrictions to others. We should ask to be filled with the Holy Spirit daily so we can take the love of God to everyone we meet. It's amazing, Jesus knew we needed a helper, so

He gave us a manifestation of the Father's love! What could be more helpful?

WHAT HOLY SPIRIT?

Through conversations with believers, I've discovered some actually undervalue the Holy Spirit's work in their ministries. Scriptural language about the Holy Spirit is often there, but the power of the Spirit can be lacking. Some believe they received all of Him when they were baptized. It isn't wrong to believe the Holy Spirit dwells in us at the moment of salvation, but to recognize this as the only moment we receive the Spirit minimizes the power He fills us with daily. In the New Testament, some believers weren't even aware there was a Holy Spirit. Acts 19:1-7 says,

"While Apollos was at Corinth, Paul took the road through the interior and arrived at Ephesus. There he found some disciples and asked them, "Did you receive the Holy Spirit when you believed?" They answered, "No, we have not even heard that there is a Holy Spirit." So Paul asked, "Then what baptism did you receive?" "John's baptism," they replied. Paul said, "John's baptism was a baptism of repentance. He told the people to believe in the one coming after him, that is, in Jesus." On hearing this, they were baptized in the name of the Lord Jesus. When Paul placed his

hands on them, the Holy Spirit came on them, and they spoke in tongues and prophesied. There were about twelve men in all."

Acts 19:1-7

We see several instances in scripture where the apostles prayed and laid their hands on those who had yet to receive the Spirit. People who followed Jesus were baptized in water, but they didn't know there was another baptism to partake in; the baptism of the Spirit. As men and women were being taught the truth about the Spirit, their minds were renewed, and they were filled with this precious gift. There are some western Christians today who have been baptized in water but have yet to be fully immersed in the gift of the Holy Spirit.

There's a tension in the modern church surrounding this topic of being filled with the Holy Spirit. While some associate this baptism with speaking in tongues, others say speaking in tongues isn't relevant. It's a dissonance between two camps often rooted in pride and deep wounds. I have a diverse religious background, so I can see and understand the viewpoint from both sides. We must meet in the middle, lay our pride and hurt aside and seek the truth about the Spirit.

There are some Christians who have taken great pride in the experience they've had speaking in tongues. Speaking in tongues is a beautiful gift, but it's nothing to be prideful about. It's a gift that we do nothing to earn. In conversation, these "spirit-filled" individuals would often insist that those who haven't spoken in tongues haven't been filled with the Spirit. This has left many Christians hurt and angry. These conversations have inflicted wounds and brought resentment, causing some to avoid deeper conversations about the Spirit.

The lack of power that we see in many western church circles is often due to this tension we see regarding the Holy Spirit. While the language regarding the Spirit is accurate, the confusion about Him sometimes causes us to set His power aside and go after different things. This is true with both sides of the spectrum. When we aren't in unity, we cripple the power of the Spirit working through us. The pride of one camp has caused religiosity, while the hurt of the other has led to resentment. When these two are working against each other, we can't walk in the body's fullness as designed.

I pray those who haven't experienced the gift of speaking in tongues will keep praying and pursuing this avenue of the Father's love. I promise it is for you! You don't have to become more spiritual to receive it, and no one is better than you because you haven't. I apologize on behalf of authentic believers if anyone has made you feel less than because you haven't spoken in tongues. It's the grace of God that lavishes it upon us. I hope you will open your mind to it and begin pursuing the Father to receive it if you haven't already.

Rather than making the Holy Spirit about tongues, I want to re-emphasize that the Spirit is about a promise of God's love being fulfilled in our lives. I've met Christians who are genuinely filled with the Spirit, who have never spoken in tongues. They're spirit-filled because they've received the gift of God's love and pursue it every day, not because they speak in supernatural languages.

This gift of love empowers us to share the Gospel. It compels us to have compassion for the lost and gives us boldness to evangelize. Just as the apostles in the book of Acts did, we can communicate the truth of the Gospel and be an effective vehicle for sharing this love with the world.

HOW DO WE RESPOND TO THE HOLY SPIRIT?

Knowing the Holy Spirit lives with us as a promise of God's love (as expressed in my earlier vision) will change how we see the apostles' response to their evangelistic mission. We notice supernatural power and boldness arise after they're filled with the Holy Spirit. They had the zeal to spread the Gospel from seeing Jesus alone, but it was the manifestation of love that now possessed them that made it their life's purpose. The constant overflow of the Spirit gave them everything they needed to finish their race well.

The Spirit empowers us the same. He is essential in our evangelism. Without Him, we're only as successful as our own efforts; and that's not much.

If we're running with the Spirit, we're moving on His terms. We are listening to the voice of God and moving where He asks us to move. Being connected to the Holy Spirit is the equivalent of a phone constantly on charge. We don't burn out or run out of juice. Sharing the Gospel is too big and delicate to handle on our own. We set ourselves up for success when we invite the Holy Spirit into our conversations with the lost. He enables us to converse with confidence, boldness, and a never-ending fountain of love.

We can glean much from the way the apostles responded to the Holy Spirit. In Acts 16, there's a powerful example of the Spirit creating an evangelistic moment through the obedience of two spirit-filled men:

"About midnight Paul and Silas were praying and singing hymns to God, and the other prisoners were listening to them. Suddenly there was such a violent earthquake that the foundations of the prison were shaken. At once all the prison doors flew open, and everyone's chains came loose. The jailer woke up, and when he saw the prison doors open, he drew his sword and was about to kill himself because he thought the prisoners had escaped. But Paul shouted, "Don't harm yourself! We are all here!" The jailer called for lights,

rushed in and fell trembling before Paul and Silas. He then brought them out and asked, "Sirs, what must I do to be saved?"

Acts 16: 25-30

While most would be overcome with fear, Paul and Silas responded with faith in the Lord. Even under physical and emotional duress, they leaned into the Spirit for direction and shared the Gospel with the prison guard. We won't see the Spirit moving in power when we let fear override our faith and obedience. When we believe the Spirit can work through us as He did through Paul and Silas, we'll be filled with power to evangelize and be a bold witness for the Lord, even in the face of persecution.

When we share the Gospel without the Spirit, people walk away without experiencing the powerful love of God. The Spirit creates space for natural healing and transformation to take place and the love of God to invade. A motivation to love is the core of evangelism. God is pleased when we allow the Spirit to empower us with love through our words and actions. The Holy Spirit is the only way we can express God's love rightly.

If we believe we're alone in sharing the Gospel, we'll approach it as so. The Spirit is with us every step. The power of the Spirit isn't something we just tap into for evangelism, living with the Holy Spirit is an experience that, once tasted, becomes a lifestyle of constant pursuit. Being filled with the Holy Spirit increases our belief that every moment is an opportunity for evangelism. A lifestyle of evangelism, at its core, is surrendering our agenda to the agenda of the Spirit. Imagine walking so closely with Him, He leads you into conversations about Jesus without you looking for them. Before you know it, He's giving you boldness, courage and spiritual gifts to evangelize with power. That's what it looks like to live an evangelistic lifestyle. We will explore more of that in chapter ten!

6

REDEEMING THE REPUTATION

Trust can be damaged in a singular instance. When you lie, cheat or say a harsh word towards someone, you may lose their trust, but a reputation is what someone becomes known for. Reputations are a culmination of events that continuously happen. I believe the shift we've experienced towards our post-Christian culture happened with time. It took many powerful acts of judgment and harmful behavior to cultivate the reputation we have with many non-believers. The church must begin a process of reconciliation. This process requires one-on-one conversations and building relationships with those hurt by the church. Our efforts in evangelism will be more successful when we destroy the reputation that precedes us.

As we've discussed, fear and feelings of insufficiency

often prevent us from sharing our faith. It's difficult to share the Gospel with someone you have no direct influence over, but it's exceedingly difficult to share with those who have a poor taste for Christianity. Experiencing hurtful behavior from people who preach the grace of Jesus has often caused resentment to the Gospel message amongst the lost.

There's a young lady, Maureen that I worked with several years ago. She's a prime example of someone hurt by the church. As I got to know Maureen and her story, I noticed there were broken places in her life surrounding Christianity. Her dad used to be an ordained minister. She grew up in a church where he was a deacon, prominent leader and had a pristine reputation with its members. Although he seemed honest and reputable, he was verbally abusive at home. He spoke with anger and hateful language to his wife while cursing and emotionally abusing his children.

His character did harmful things to his family, especially Maureen. She developed resentment, not only towards her dad, but towards all Christian's. It was hard hearing Maureen's heart through her brokenness. To know that a man of faith could cause so much hatred towards Christians was baffling. Having these tough conversations with Maureen allowed me to see some of those tattered places in her heart and speak truth into them. Someone like

Maureen doesn't just give an open ear to any Christian she meets. It takes trust and relationship to begin healing in hearts like hers. The devil has many ways of speaking lies over us. When Christians misrepresent God by living out of alignment with His character, like Maureen's father, we partner with the enemy in advancing his evil agenda.

Maureen's story isn't foreign to you. You have friends and loved ones who are rowing in the same boat she is. Deep wounds and hurt from the church have left them stranded in a sea of deception. God is calling us to swim out and bring them back home. Without seeing something different on the land they came from, they'll never desire to go back. An encounter of love and compassion is the only thing that will give them hope that the Lord differs from what they originally experienced.

This chapter isn't a bashing session against the church or Christians, but we should be aware of the pain that has been caused by many believers. As post-Christian evangelists, we have a responsibility to initiate the healing process among those who have been hurt by the church. Many non-believers have been wounded so deeply, they often despise having conversations about Christianity or God at all. It's more important, now than ever, to test our character and align our behavior with the heart of God. It's when we love and care the way Jesus does that these wounds will be healed, and lives will be surrendered to the Lord.

RECEPTIVITY TO RESISTANCE - THE SCALE

In their book *Unchristian*, Dave Kinnaman and Gabe Lyons introduce a scale from one to ten that shows us the receptivity to evangelism in our post-Christian context. Ten represents a great receptivity to hearing and believing the Gospel while zero represents a greater resistance. In the early eighties and nineties, evangelism wasn't resisted as heavily as it is now. Kinnaman and Lyons placed non-believers during this time at an eight. Non-believers found conversations about Christianity more intriguing, and they engaged a little easier. Individuals didn't have resentment towards the church to the extent they do today, creating fewer filters that lead to resistance to the Gospel.

They now claim that non-believers in general have moved from an eight on this scale, to a three. That's a substantial drop. As many non-believers have been hurt by the church, they've become less receptive to conversing about Jesus. Understanding this will change how we talk to non-believers. It also gives us a reality check that something must change to reverse the reputation we have with the world. I believe we are heading in a positive direction of restoration, but we still have work to do. Church leaders and Christians alike are aware of the hurt the church has caused and haven't taken it lightly. We are seeing a trend back towards greater receptivity.

In this chapter, we'll discuss starting this process of

restoration and things we can do to help soften the heart of those less receptive. Think of those you know who have been wounded by the church. Place yourself in their shoes as you read along and imagine how they feel about Christianity and the church. When we identify with the pain people endure, we may not receive the solution to fix it, but we'll gain the empathy to share Jesus with them. He can heal their hearts and renew their minds. There are people in your life that you can build closer relationships with to show the authentic love of God. Here are a few key things to help you cultivate those intimate relationships.

Empathy

Empathy is required to begin this process of healing. Think back to my friend Maureen. After building a relationship with her at work, she finally let me in on the hurt she had experienced in her earlier years. She is somewhat a reserved person, so she doesn't open up to people very easily. She felt comfortable sharing those parts of her with me because she trusted that I genuinely cared about her. Empathy opens the door to allow those who have been hurt to become vulnerable with us. Some people are more resistant and skeptical than others, so it may take more time to build the relationship, but they will open up when they believe you care for them.

It's one thing to tell someone you care about them, it's

another to show it. One way I show others I care for them is to simply listen. We can often be so quick to tell our story, we forget to listen to someone else tell theirs. Empathy requires an understanding of someone's emotions and connecting to how they feel on some level. We must be intentional about listening to what they say and how they feel. I've found people who have been healed from their wounds are exceptional conversationalists with others who have been hurt. They know what it's like to feel pain and how to listen to someone talk about theirs. Listening is one of the more powerful ways we can empathize.

Maybe you haven't been hurt to a large extent by the church, and that's okay. You can still empathize with those who have. Remember, it isn't your job to decide whether their pain is valid, and it isn't fair to assume they process things like you. Just listen and know that they feel pain, even if you feel it's unreasonable. Empathy doesn't give us all the answers. That's not what people need. Hurt people need someone they can talk to and open up with. When you empathize with someone, you create an avenue for the healing process to begin.

Apologetic

When building relationships or evangelizing to those who have been hurt, we should be ready to ask forgiveness on behalf of the church. I've discovered that an apology goes a long way. Asking for forgiveness does two things. First, it gives someone hope that what they've experienced wasn't genuine Christianity. Second, it provides an opportunity for them to forgive so their heart can heal. Apologies often cause us to swallow pride, but it can be a big blow to the glass that covers someone's heart. An apology could shatter it and allow them to receive the goodness of God.

The ones who have church wounds have nothing against you. You just happen to represent someone from their past who inflicted them with pain. When you apologize on behalf of the church, you are standing in the one's place who initially caused this hurt. This is what Jesus did on the cross for us. He took the apology for the fall of man and carried it as His own. The Lord may ask us to step in and ask forgiveness, but we should gladly carry that weight, knowing it could open the door for someone's restoration.

To be effective in sharing the Gospel, we must recognize when the church's behavior is out of alignment with the character of Jesus and be ready to own up to it. It's not enough to just apologize. People will only trust an apology until they feel nothing has changed. To be a vessel in someone's healing process, we must show them that there is a better way than what they previously experienced.

Another Way

Actions always speak louder than words. The apology is the start, but true healing comes when the truth is brought forth and experienced. What good would it do for us to apologize and not change our behavior? After we instill hope that there is something better about Christianity, we must show them. Jesus is our best example of what this looks like:

"But Jesus went to the Mount of Olives. At dawn he appeared again in the temple courts, where all the people gathered around him, and he sat down to teach them. The teachers of the law and the Pharisees brought in a woman caught in adultery. They made her stand before the group and said to Jesus, "Teacher, this woman was caught in the act of adultery. In the Law Moses commanded us to stone such women. Now what do you say?" They were using this question as a trap, in order to have a basis for accusing him. But Jesus bent down and started to write on the ground with his finger. When they kept on questioning him, he straightened up and said to them, "Let any one of you who is without sin be the first to throw a stone at her." Again, he stooped down and wrote on the ground. At this, those who heard began to go away one at a time, the older ones first, until only Jesus was left, with the woman still standing there. Jesus straightened up and asked her, "Woman, where are they? Has no one condemned you?"

"No one, sir," she said. "Then neither do I condemn you," Jesus declared. "Go now and leave your life of sin."

John 8:1-11

It was common in this day for women to be persecuted after being caught in acts of sexual idolatry. It would be normal for this woman to expect a death sentence. The religious leaders knew no other option. Since Jesus claimed to be the coming Messiah, the leaders thought they would interrupt His teaching to see what He had to say. It wasn't justice they were seeking in bringing this woman to Jesus, they wanted to make a mockery of Him and His authority. They were aiming to prove to the crowds they were right, and He was wrong. Jesus was unlike anyone they'd ever seen. He represented a form of justice more gracious than the law they knew.

A religious spirit chooses to be right over building relationships. Genuine compassion draws us into connection with others and allows us to extend mercy when it seems more fitting to punish. I'm reminded so often of the mercy Jesus gave on the cross. He paid for the death I deserved, and now it's my joy to extend mercy to others. The religious leaders never experienced this affection from the Lord. By clinging to their pride and fighting for legalistic justice, they missed the extravagance of the Lord's presence among them. Jesus didn't desire to tell the Pharisees they were wrong; His intent was in showing everyone there was a better way.

It's vital we show the hurt and afflicted this better way. Scripture reminds us that the kindness of the Lord brings us to repentance. Those who have been wounded by the church often feel they've been wrongfully judged and condemned. We have the honor to connect them to the One who can bring true repentance. We do this through our grace, understanding, and kindness.

Broken things aren't mended by the methods that initially break them. You can't throw pieces of a shattered vase on the floor and expect it to be restored; therefore, we can't help these broken people heal through our religiosity and harsh judgment. By building relationships and letting the Lord's character flow from us, we can show those who have been hurt by the church this better way.

THE OVERFLOW OF GRACE

The grace we give differs greatly from the grace of Jesus. In our fleshly minds, we often limit our outpouring of grace to the ones we feel deserve it or those we feel will respond to it. We treat it as an investment to spend wisely rather than an endless stream of love to give lavishly. The prevenient grace of God constantly pokes the hearts of the lost before He invites us into their situations. By refusing to extend our grace to everyone, we deny that the Spirit is already there, doing a work. The Father's grace is a continuous fountain; it never slows down, and it never ruins dry. We tend to cling to the faucet to disrupt that flow when we feel our grace will return void. It should be our desire that God would create in us an ever-flowing fountain like His. When we're genuinely connected to the source, we'll never want that flow to stop.

In Luke 17, we see the story of the ten lepers. After they shout to Jesus in desperation for healing, He tells them to go show themselves to the priest and they would be healed. When they were healed, only one returned to Jesus to thank Him for His mercy. The other nine went on their way, not returning to thank Jesus for what He'd done.

So often, we take holy moments for granted. Just as the nine ungrateful lepers, it's not rare for the generosity and kindness of the Lord to slip my mind. I can never truly give the Lord the praise and thanksgiving He deserves, but that didn't stop Him from dying on a cross for me. God is all-knowing. He was aware of the ones who wouldn't come back to thank Him, but He healed them anyway. The assumed response to our grace should never be the reason we extend it to the world. Jesus didn't have an agenda in healing the ten lepers, He was simply obeying the Father and creating a moment for them to draw closer to Him. That should be our heart for evangelism.

You may feel you make an impact in one out of every ten people you tell about the Lord. When extending love is the only agenda, you will never fail. Never underestimate the power of the Holy Spirit to move, even amongst "the least of these." Those you feel have zero chance of responding to your message have a purpose in building the Kingdom just like you and me. The grace and love you present to them may be what the Holy Spirit has prepared them to receive. Your act of obedience could be the final blow that uncovers their eyes to see Jesus and their Kingdom identity and purpose.

It's tricky to put language to what God's grace looks like. It's more tangible in how we receive it than how we explain it. His motive for evangelism runs deeper in grace for the unbeliever than ours do. To be effective evangelists, we should align our hearts and motives with those of the Lord. In our post-Christian culture, where church hurt and spiritual wounds run rampant, we should be eager to tell others about Jesus with grace and kindness. Instead, we often hold it inside and wait for the right person to come along. I urge you to give it freely. Jesus died for you when you were still a slave to sin. Our response should be one with similar motives when evangelizing to the lost.

FIGHTING TO BE HEARD

Because many believers have inflicted hurt upon the lost, our voice has gotten smaller in influencing society. People truly don't care how much you know until they know how much you care. When we lack empathy, we stunt the Gospel message from impacting those around us. We must fight to regain our influence. It's our Christlike character that will help redeem our reputation and give our voice influence in society once again. There must be a connection made that softens the heart of the nonbeliever to bend an ear to our message.

Ravi Zacharias says, "If the method of evangelism is in violation of its message, people will sniff it out quickly." When we share our faith with others, our character must align with the message we are preaching. Without it, people will sniff out our agenda and close their ears to hear what we have to say. When people sense we aren't authentic with what we preach, they will write us off. Peter says in 1 Peter 3:15, "but in your hearts revere Christ as Lord. Always be prepared to give an answer to everyone who asks you to give the reason for the hope that you have. But do this with gentleness and respect." Other translations use the word kindness in place of gentleness. Peter knew the power of being kind to those we share our faith with. Supernatural healing and receptivity happen when kindness flows from the believer. A lifestyle of kindness and compassion is essential in showing our authentic love and regaining our influence in our current society.

Relational evangelism is an effective way to extend

our voice to the lost. It's effective because that's how we were designed and instructed to share the Gospel. Our relationships should never be a means to an end, but through them, we build trust and gain influence to share the Gospel. Relational evangelism doesn't mean we only evangelize to our friends, it means we relationally connect to everyone we meet.

Connecting relationally can always be improved upon. We want to put our best foot forward in our evangelistic efforts. This requires a desire to learn and improve in the areas in which we struggle. In the next chapter, we will look at some practical ways we can initiate and deepen our conversations relationally. Through genuine empathy for the lost, finding common ground and forming intentional connections, we point others from all walks of life to the heart of Jesus.

WORD OF KNOWLEDGE IN A LAUNDROMAT

A memorable moment of evangelism for me was one of the first times I experienced the risk of stepping out in faith. I was new to the gifts of the Holy Spirit, specifically words of knowledge. At the time, I was with my youth group handing out money at a coin laundromat to bless strangers. I interacted with a few people as one of the small group leaders shared the Gospel. I could have never predicted what would come next. I approached a gentleman who looked worn out from the day. He was wearing a uniform like that of a mechanic. I handed him some coins, and he gladly took the money. Without saying thanks, he asked if I had more. Initially, his response startled me. The Lord spoke to my heart that someone had wronged him and stolen money. I answered no to his question of more money. I wrestled continuing the conversation, but finally asked if someone had wronged him recently. He didn't say anything but looked at me as if I were right. I felt more confidence and asked if someone had stolen money from him. He then looked at me as if to say, "how do you know?" He began to get paranoid and started looking around. He questioned if I was a cop. Immediately, I explained who I was and the deep concern of the Father's heart for him. The man listened intently as I began to break down forgiveness and the power of letting go. At this point, he moved to some chairs and sat down. I could see that his mind was racing. I kept urging him and encouraging him that this moment was divine. I could feel the tension in the atmosphere as the Lord wanted to invade this man's situation with heaven. Unfortunately, I didn't see him reach mercy because our group's time there was coming to an end. As we left, I felt the Lord give more clarity that he was wronged in a drug deal and money was stolen. The man was ready to take action into his own hands, even considering murder. This moment of evangelism let me experience the Father's heart in a fresh way outside of a church service. It made me hunger more for His voice. He treasures His lost children, and I felt the depth of His concern. I believe this man was marked by this divine intervention.

-Sangley

7

GETTING PRACTICAL IN OUR CONVERSATIONS

Growing up, I would occasionally go out with a group from church to knock on doors and evangelize. This was a part of a monthly outreach ministry designed to invite people to church. We'd often find a neighborhood and walk from house to house, sharing the Gospel. This wasn't something I enjoyed doing. It made me feel tremendous anxiety as a child. I've learned recently this method of evangelism still makes me feel very uncomfortable.

Several weeks ago, I went to a nearby store to evangelize with a group of close friends. I found it difficult to start random conversations with strangers. While some of my friends felt comfortable in this method of evangelism, I did not. I'm more of an "ease-into-the-conversation" kind of guy. Finding common ground and slowly making my way into a conversation is where I feel most comfortable. I'm sure many of you can relate. It's okay to not be one who is good at randomly approaching someone to share your faith. Each personality is unique, and we all have different strengths.

There is hope that we can become more efficient in the areas we aren't strong in. I felt unsuccessful in an area of evangelism I have little experience in. That doesn't mean I can't be great at it. I look forward to the next time we go! I want to grow in my areas of weakness!

There are countless ways to become a better evangelist. Like anything else, evangelism takes practice and persistent work. It won't be easy and sometimes will seem unsuccessful. I want to assure you, it's okay. If evangelism was easy and always left you feeling good, everyone would do it. It's encouraging that we can always get better. We can always press into the Lord to help us share His message more effectively. He wants us to lean into Him to teach us how to relate with others and be humble carriers of the Gospel.

Preparing ourselves for evangelism is the first step in becoming intentional evangelists. Starting conversations about Jesus without a plan is scary. We trust the guidance of the Holy Spirit, but good preparation will allow us to see opportunities and give us the confidence to navigate conversations fluently. Just as we prepare to make the basketball team or land a big interview, we should strive for excellence in our efforts to evangelize.

I want to focus on some practical ways we can get better at evangelizing relationally. I'm a firm believer that our post-Christian culture requires more of this method of evangelism. As discussed in the last chapter, there's a healing process that must take place for many non-believers to entertain following Christ. Connecting relationally is the avenue I believe will lead to this healing. Relationship doesn't mean you wait five years to evangelize, it means you connect with those you meet and show them a better way! It can happen over time, or it can happen walking through the grocery store. We prepare well when we become intentional about connecting in relational ways.

THE RIGHT PLACE AT THE RIGHT TIME

If you've been active in the church for any length of time, you may find many of your friends are believers. We tend to hang out with other Christians because we need a spiritual community in our lives. It's also natural for us to hang out with people just like us. I've often found we cling so tight to believers because it's comfortable, but in order to evangelize to the lost, we must learn to break out of our

Christian bubbles. How can we tell the lost about Jesus if we never plan to hang out with them?

I have a friend who loves the card game, *Magic*. One or two times a week, he will meet at a local card shop to play with individuals from all walks of life. It's not only fun and competitive for him, but he also uses it as an avenue for evangelism. He's a pastor who loves his congregation, but he also enjoys ministering to those who don't know Jesus. He has positioned himself well to build relationships and talk to non-believers about his faith.

Using our hobbies to build relationships is one way to be intentional about sharing the Gospel. You may enjoy kayaking, so join a kayaking club. You may even want to take karate classes on the weekends. There are many activities you can take part in that will open opportunities to build relationships. Think about some ways you can expose yourself to non-believers regularly. It doesn't have to be an activity you enjoy or club you join, it can be a place you like to go. Connecting relationally could result from eating inside instead of going through a drive thru. It's easy to build relationships when you are intentional and have a purpose in doing so.

I love to read, write and watch sports. These are my go-to pleasures, but I can do them alone and be perfectly fine. I found I would often hermit in my room while I binged Netflix or read a book. It was comfortable for me to sit at my desk to write or watch a football game.

To be intentional about evangelizing, I began taking my computer to a local Starbucks or Chick-Fil-A to position myself around other people. In doing this, I've had many opportunities to talk and build relationships with strangers. Occasionally, I've been able to speak about spiritual matters and share the Gospel with the lost. The regulars I've met now know my name and that I'm working on a book about Jesus. Sometimes they ask how it's going or ask questions about God. Because I have positioned and prepared myself well, I now have opportunities to build relationships and converse with people about life and Jesus. This wouldn't have happened if I'd never left my room.

Andy Stanley once told a story of him and his family going to the beach and intentionally looking for sharks' teeth. As they kept their head down and focused on the shoreline, they saw them everywhere. He said they found a bucket full. Before that trip, he had never seen a shark's tooth lying on the beach in his life. When we become intentional about finding something, we are more apt to find it. The same goes for evangelism. When we look for someone to share the Gospel story with, we will always find them. If we become intentional about relationally connecting, we will see opportunities for evangelism arise all around us.

HIGH EXPECTANCY

Not only should we expect opportunities to arise, we should be expectant of what God will do through them. If we expect that supernatural transformation and healing will happen, we'll be more receptive to the things the Spirit is doing in our conversations. I never want to enter an evangelistic conversation believing little of what can happen. Conversations won't always be flawless. Just because we have high hopes and faith in the Lord doesn't mean there won't be genuine moments of disappointment and learning. Our expectancy for the Lord to reveal His power aligns our heart to reveal the kindness and grace of God in every situation, no matter the outcome.

This past summer, I traveled to Los Angeles for a mission trip. I've always loved reading stories about people witnessing on planes. It may be because of my desire to travel, but something about it just fascinates me. As I was getting ready for my trip, I would constantly pray about the person I would sit next to on my flight to LA. The more I prayed in preparation for this trip, the higher my expectancy became that God would do a powerful work in my conversations during travel.

As I boarded the plane that morning, I looked back to get a preview of who I'd be sitting next to. I noticed a little girl and her mom sitting in my row. I'd been expectant for months that the Lord would use me powerfully. As I sat down, the little girl started a conversation with me! She had one of those spunky personalities that would talk to anyone who would listen. We hit it off, immediately.

We talked a long time about movies and other things she enjoyed. I spoke with her mom for a while regarding their business in Los Angeles. As we talked, I spoke to the Lord and asked him to reveal things to me about this family. I asked Him to open a door for me to insert Him into the conversation. As I kept praying, the mom kept telling me pieces of their story. She said she felt at peace about sharing those areas with me.

Amid my conversation with them, the mom revealed that she had a close friend diagnosed with a troubling condition that could be fatal in the next several years. I had discovered that they were also Christians and I asked if I could pray for healing over that sickness. It was as a powerful moment as they were encouraged in the Lord for their friend's future. We also talked about many other things regarding their spiritual journeys. They were also very encouraging in my endeavors in LA. I may never know the outcome of their friend's situation, but because of my expectancy and preparation, I was positioned to hear from the Lord and minister to this family powerfully.

Expecting for more than the things we have already seen also places us in an influential position to minister. No matter where we are in our spiritual journey, God can always do more.

Several months ago, I was asked to lead worship for a friend's youth revival. In talking with him to prepare for the event, he mentioned this group had never experienced supernatural manifestations of the Holy Spirit in their services. Words of knowledge and prophecy weren't a high expectancy for this group; however, I felt the Lord wanted to do abundantly more. I admit I have often fell victim to going with the flow of a ministry's culture, but I resisted and let the Lord have His way.

The first couple of nights, I asked the Lord to reveal specific areas about some of these students' lives. I kept praying for compassion and revelation for them. On my way home the second night, He began revealing specific dreams pertaining to a young gentleman I had met that night. I immediately pulled over and jotted everything down on my phone. I planned to share these things with him the following service.

The next night, as I sat down to listen to the message being preached, the Lord began revealing things to me regarding one of the high school ladies there as well. After service, I pulled her and a leader to the side and shared with her the things given to me. It's always humbling to see identity being solidified through a prophetic word. I could see the anticipation in her soul for the things being revealed.

I found out at the end of the night the two students I received words for were brother and sister. On the last night, I ministered with the young man and invited his sister to stand with him. She grabbed his hand, and they both began agreeing and believing together. When I got done, they both had tears streaming down their faces, and so did I. He couldn't say anything, but his sister spoke up for him. She said what I revealed were things they had stopped believing in for their family a long time ago. She now believed more confidently they would see them come to fruition. This is my favorite story to tell and reflect on. We will never stop seeing an increase in God's power when we believe there is always more He wants to offer.

THE NO-FAIL PLAN

As we have discussed, the only agenda of evangelism is to share the love of God with someone. There may be times where you feel as if you've failed in sharing the Gospel. You may get heavy pushback, or someone may not respond the way you had hoped. It's normal for those things to happen. In our preparation, it's important to know that when we evangelize from a place of compassion and love as Jesus does, we can't fail. The love of God will always succeed. His love is the ultimate no-fail plan.

FINDING COMMON GROUND

Starting conversations can be difficult. We can alleviate this pressure when we find a similarity first. There are several ways we can find common ground when evangelizing. The story I mentioned earlier of my friend using a card game as an avenue to evangelize is just one of them. Surrounding yourself with people who enjoy doing the same things you do is one of the best ways to find similarities and build relationships.

One way you have probably already practiced finding common ground is in dating. First dates usually consist of general questions that find close similarities. Finding common ground with strangers isn't all that different. When you meet someone new, it's normal to ask them questions to learn things about their life. When you find a mutual interest, feed off of that to take the conversation deeper. You may have found a sweet spot!

In my earlier story, I discovered that I wasn't good at starting conversations with random people at the grocery store. Finding common ground with them first helps me ease into the conversation. After I begin a conversation, things flow naturally for me. One way I have gotten good at finding common ground is by going to areas where I have an array of knowledge. This usually involves me just doing things that I already do, but with an intention to evangelize.

For example, when I am in Walmart, I often browse in

the book section, the electronic department or over by the Legos. These are all things I enjoy doing and have enough knowledge to start a conversation. One of my go-to places is a local bookstore. I meet unique people there. A side note though, unless I am browsing for myself, I like to stay away from the Christian section. I like to go to the business or sports sections where I might meet someone who doesn't know the Lord. You can usually start a conversation with someone when you notice they have a similar interest as you. Go to those places often to create those evangelistic opportunities.

BE OBSERVANT

Sometimes finding common ground can be a little tricky. Creativity will help you start a conversation when it seems there's nothing in common. Compliments are one of the easiest ways. It takes little to offer a nice compliment to someone. When you give a compliment, it not only begins a small conversation, but it opens them up to be receptive to your kindness.

It's also easy to notice things you know or enjoy. If you love dogs, ask to pet someone's dog. If you notice someone wearing a LeBron James jersey and you like basketball, go talk about basketball. There are so many ways we can start small conversations when we notice obvious things about people.

Be intentional about having conversation pieces on you. Starting a conversation doesn't always have to begin with you. Sometimes you can lure people to start one themselves. I have a handful of stickers on my computer of things I like. People often approach me and strike up a conversation because they see one they have an interest in. I've also had people start conversations with me about sports attire I was wearing. They didn't know it, but they walked into a conversation where the Holy Spirit would be present. How cool is that? Be creative. You will find different ways that work for you in helping you start a conversation.

In my office at work, I have a Los Angeles poster on my wall. Why would a quiet conservative boy from Georgia have a poster of LA? Funny you should ask, everyone else does too!

Los Angeles has garnished a very special place in my heart from the time I have spent there doing mission work. Whenever someone asks me about the poster, it initiates a conversation for me to talk about the opportunity I had there. It's a conversation that sets itself up. I have engaged in powerful conversations about the Lord through that poster. It doesn't take much to create opportunities like this. There are always unique ways you can set yourself up to have these conversations.

By being intentional, we can create conversations that

aren't there to the naked eye. With awareness and the heart of an evangelist, we can turn those conversations into life-transforming moments. It isn't easy to strike up conversations with strangers, but when we take an initiative to get better, we trust the Lord to take us out of our social comfort zones and lead us into those conversations.

TAKING THE CONVERSATION DEEPER BY ASKING GOOD QUESTIONS

Starting a conversation is only half the battle. When we meet someone new or build a trusting relationship, we want to take our conversations to a deeper level. Deeper conversations won't happen if you're interested in only talking about sports or Lego's. We want to create more meaningful conversations so the Lord can work in the deeper areas of someone's heart. We can always take the conversation deeper when we learn the art of asking good questions.

Find Out Their Background

Asking questions about someone's background is usually acceptable after you establish common ground. People are naturally created to connect, so being intrigued by someone's life isn't unusual. When you ask questions about someone's past, you get an insight into where they've been and what has shaped them. Some may be closed off, and that's okay. If you feel pushback, just know they have some places they may not feel comfortable talking about. These situations may require more trust and a deeper relationship.

Questions like "Where are you from?" or "Where did you graduate?" will often open up more conversation about their past. Knowing some of their past will help you connect Jesus to their future. As they reveal things to you, opportunities may arise to take the conversation deeper, so just listen. It will also show you how receptive they may be to a spiritual conversation. Be attentive to their story and the Holy Spirit, of course.

Dreams and Goals

Passionate people enjoy talking about their plans. When you engage in conversation with someone, discovering what they hope to accomplish will give you an indication of what drives them and what they find most valuable in life. I love conversations where I can connect Jesus to someone's future. Jesus loves our passions and our dreams. I believe He wants to use the things we are passionate about to build His Kingdom.

I was speaking to a gentleman once who I knew wasn't a Christian. As he answered questions regarding his hopes and aspirations, I could tell he was very passionate about the things he wanted to do. He had a longing for feeding the hungry and helping the poor. With some good questions, I discovered He didn't know Jesus. His desire to help the needy was one of humanism, not the love of the Lord in his heart.

Through the conversation, I connected him with a local ministry that did much of what he was passionate about. I shared with him how Jesus had a heart for doing the same things. I shared the Gospel story with him right there. He now knows the story of Jesus and how they both share the same desires for the less fortunate. I pray as he continues to connect these dots and become more familiar with the story of Jesus, he will accept Him into his heart.

Cause Them to Think

As you find out more about someone's life, you can move into conversations that involve the deeper areas of their heart. When you converse with people long enough, they'll reveal things that made large impacts on their life. You may hear about losing a prestigious job or a family member. Some will tell you about big achievements or awards. You may even hear about divorces or relationship problems. Count nothing out.

When you see that they are talking about something meaningful to them, you can go deeper. Questions like, "How did you handle that?" or "How did that make you feel?" will cause them to process their thoughts right in front of you. When this happens, you may be given the opportunity to become a voice in their response. Questions like these often allow you to hear broken places or coping mechanisms that provide moments to insert the truth of the Gospel. When people think out loud, it can often allow us to interject our own thoughts. When your thoughts are pure and Gospel-centered, you've uncovered an evangelistic opportunity.

You will discover on your own more questions you can use that allow people to think out loud. Remember, the agenda is love and compassion, not moving through a process of conversation. It's not a dogmatic step-by-step method of evangelism. Each person is unique and carries something special. Listen to their heart and ask the Lord for compassion and wisdom. These practical tools don't matter if love isn't the overarching goal.

You can practice initiating and going deeper into conversations. Start small and keep working at it. With every conversation we have about the Lord, He wants to do something powerful. He desires to connect a person's heart with His and transform it forever. We've been chosen to partake in these beautiful interactions. Let's carry that responsibility and strive for excellence as post-Christian evangelists!

Say you have built trust in a relationship or conversation and have asked good questions to discover the depths of someone's heart. What now? Keep in mind, being relational with someone isn't pushy or agenda-driven, but we want to connect the truth of Jesus to someone's situation. That means we must know the truth and how to communicate it in everyday conversations. In the next chapter, we will discuss more practicalities to inject the truth of the Gospel into the encounters with those you meet.

8

THE GOSPEL CONVERSATION

Many Christians all over the world have fears regarding evangelism. One being they aren't qualified to be evangelists. We often carry a false assumption that the more knowledge we have about the Bible or God, the better we are at being a Christian. Insecurities rise with a lack of knowledge or the possibility of not being able to answer hard questions. These insecurities hinder our evangelism, making us believe we aren't good enough to do it.

We shouldn't back away from evangelism because we feel we aren't qualified. Even if we believe we may not be good at evangelism, stepping into it will allow us to get better. Where's the excitement in only doing things we're good at? I have always enjoyed taking jobs or signing up for roles I felt unqualified for. I find it challenging and rewarding when I get better and see the areas I underestimated myself in. There was much fear of not being qualified in writing this book, but I knew I couldn't let that stop me. The Lord takes our weaknesses and uses them to show how powerful He is. So, if you feel insecure in sharing the Gospel, you are in the best position to step up to the plate!

When the Lord commands us to do something and then gives us what we need to do it, we're qualified. Sure, there may be a lot you don't know about God or scripture, but you know your story. That's all you need to share the hope that lives inside of you. This road of evangelism, just like any other, is a process of learning. As you continue to share the Gospel, you will gain knowledge and perspective through experience and you will become a great evangelist!

While we are qualified to evangelize, that shouldn't stop us from being teachable. I approach every conversation as an opportunity to learn something new. While knowledge doesn't qualify us to evangelize, we should always want to know more about God and His Word. You'll be evangelizing too many who have questions and disbelief regarding Christianity. We always want to be in a process of learning so we can answer those questions with confidence when they arise.

We've talked about how to connect, build trust, and

take our conversations deeper. This chapter will focus on the spiritual areas of our conversations. We'll go over some aspects of our faith we should anticipate discussing with non-believers. We will also explore some difficult questions that often arise and different ways we hear from the Lord as we speak with others. We can't assume that non-believers know much about Christianity, so there are areas we should be ready to discuss regarding what we believe.

THE ROAD TO SALVATION

When I was a teenager, I had a youth pastor give me a Bible with five or six tabs placed on specific verses within its pages. After he handed these Bibles to our group, he took us from one tab to the next. He explained when we follow them in order, they would provide us with the biblical road to salvation. They were the key verses to know in leading someone to Christ. He was emphatic that we carry that Bible around to always be ready for evangelistic opportunities.

I've thought about that Bible often over the past 18 years. I recently searched some old boxes to find it, to no avail. As much as I think a tool like that Bible can be productive, I want to be sure we aren't making our Gospel message a presentation. I want the truths we know about our faith to be written on our hearts, not tabbed in a Bible for easy access. While it's not a bad idea to use a Bible during a conversation, and at times necessary, I believe we can be more relational in sharing the Gospel when it's not a routine process. We can make a bigger impact when the Word of God flows through us instead of us thumbing through a Bible, trying to find the right scripture. Our message should be a conversation, not a presentation.

I want to give you my brief version of the road to salvation. These are a couple of truths you can touch on while sharing the Gospel with a non-believer. I won't ask you to take this book with you and use this section as you share, but it's important to have a game plan as you guide non-believers through biblical truths.

This isn't a rigid process. The following are just a few basic truths you will need to know to help a non-believer understand the simple Gospel. When you connect the dots between these events, you can explore with them how the Gospel story relates to their lives and current situations. Each conversation will flow differently, and it's important to hear from the Holy Spirit and go with that flow. There may be areas you find you use more than others and some you want to add that you feel comfortable sharing. That's okay. Find the truths you can speak on with conviction. Here are just a few key truths I refer to in evangelical conversations often.

The Garden

We want to create things perfectly the first time through. When we have a vision for something, we desire for the product to be just as we envisioned. The story of our creation is no different. God had a vision for us and breathed us into existence with no flaws. We must emphasize the way God originally created us. Many Christians today focus on their sinful nature as the beginning of their story. If we don't know where we started, we'll never comprehend what He is restoring us to. He created us in His image; the way He desired us. He planned to reconcile us back to our original state of being, which was perfect communion with Him.

The Fall of Man

It's difficult for many to grasp why the fall happened. If God made everything perfect, how did man fall into sin?

Because God is the definition of love, He created us out of His love for us. Love isn't manipulative or controlling. The fall happened because man had a choice to obey God's command and failed to do so. After Adam and Eve ate the fruit, they were no longer in perfect communion with the Father as originally intended. A chasm was placed between God and man, and we lost our direct access to Him. For all have sinned and fall short of the Glory of God. Romans. (Rom 3:23) This void between us required a plan to be put into place to redeem us back into relationship with the Father.

The Messiah is Born

Biblical scholars estimate there were 4000 years between creation and the birth of Jesus. In this time, we see many Fathers of the faith who still influence us today. We also see moments of God's wrath over those who constantly refused to turn from their sin. All this time, God had a plan for redemption.

The religious leaders were on the lookout for the coming Messiah, but they never expected it to be a baby born in a wooden manger. How Jesus came to earth shattered everyone's expectations and resisted the religious hierarchy in current operation. The Messiah was expected to come from royalty. What better way to redeem God's children back to Him than through His own Son? The Messiah was born, and God's plan for reconciliation was put into place.

Death, Burial, and Resurrection

Because there was a wrong that needed correction, the perfect heir of His Kingdom had to sacrifice Himself to make a way for redemption. Scripture tells us Jesus became sin so we could become the righteousness of God (2 Cor 5:21). Jesus was humiliated as He died the death we deserved. Our sinful nature was nailed on the cross to die with Jesus and buried in the grave with Him. As Jesus came out of the grave, we rose with Him as the righteousness of God. Through the sacrifice of Jesus and His resurrection, we were once again given access to the Father.

I encourage you, as Paul instructs, to work out your salvation among yourself with fear and trembling. Know these aspects of the Gospel story and how they have transformed your own life. Be ready to share that as you explore these areas with non-believers. When they see how the Gospel has transformed your life, they will be more open to letting it transform theirs as well!

WHAT MUST WE DO?

So, what happens when someone wants to become a Christian? What does scripture say regarding salvation? It's simple. Believe in your hearts and confess with your mouth that Jesus is Lord, and you will be saved (Rom 10: 9-10). So often, we've made salvation about saying a prayer with our mouths and we've missed the heart portion of this scripture.

Believing in our hearts and confessing with our mouths that Jesus is Lord is the simplicity of the Gospel. Each conversion is different. Every person has a unique salvation story!

A friend once told me an experience where the

sinner's prayer looked a little different than it had before. He was ministering to a girl on the street side in his hometown and was speaking new life and identity over her. She decided that she wanted to follow Christ! She mentioned she'd never imagined following Jesus before and didn't know the next step. My friend gently grabbed her hand and said, "As we take this step together, believe and put your faith and trust in the Lord and you will be saved." They took one large step forward and the young girl was overwhelmed with emotion and love for the Lord. She then proclaimed softly, "I love you, Jesus!" She put her faith in the Lord in that very moment without saying the prayer you and I may have become accustomed to! Listen to the Spirit and He will show you how to usher someone into a relationship with the Lord!

THE SCARIEST THING FOR ME

The scariest thing for me while sharing the Gospel is being asked hard questions I don't have the answers to. Unfortunately, some non-believers believe if you don't know every detail about God, then your account for Him is discredited. We know this isn't true but being aware that some think this way should urge us to search the Bible apologetically and be ready to help their unbelief.

I mentioned earlier an instance I had at work where I was asked what my beliefs were regarding dinosaurs' existence on earth. Out of every question I thought I may get stumped on, I never thought it would be dinosaurs. The person who asked me this question found it admirable when I told her I didn't know and that I would look into an answer for her. The reason she was so curious about that question was because it was a hang-up for her husband. She said he found it outrageous that dinosaurs lived billions of years ago, but the timeline for the Christian faith didn't line up with that discovery. Because of this, he threw Christianity to the side as a false belief system.

Many non-believers have those hang-ups. One idea or inconsistency can often throw people off from being receptive to the good news. Although this is heartbreaking, it gives me a lot of hope. What if I can be the one to step into a conversation and provide an answer for someone's hang-up? What if that one answer breaks through the glass of their heart, and they follow Jesus for eternity? That's the reason I share the Gospel; to give people the truth where they are lacking and to aid in replacing it with the hope of Jesus.

People will ask hard questions. It's okay to not have all the answers, but we should always seek the truth about what we believe. I want to present some questions I've discovered to be popular for non-believers to ask. I also want to give a general answer to them. Be diligent in seeking the truth about what you believe. This evangelistic journey is a process. More questions will arise with time that you must seek answers to. Here are some I've come across. If someone asks you a question and you don't have the answer, tell them you don't know and give them the hope of Jesus inside of you instead!

THE HARD QUESTIONS

If God is Real, Why Do Bad Things Happen?

There was a season I struggled with this question too. I couldn't imagine why a mighty and powerful God wouldn't put His hand on a bad situation to stop it from being bad. My two brothers grew up with a disease I knew would eventually take their lives. I asked God persistently if He would remove it from them. I wanted so badly for Him to bring healing to their lives. He never did, and I fought with why for a long time.

People have seen a world full of sickness, violence and corruption. It's easy to understand why faith in God is lacking when we see negative situations not being turned around. It's not until we're taught good theology that we'll believe that God is still good. Through the pain, suffering and animosity, the truth of God and His deity will give us the faith to believe that He is real and active, even in the worst circumstances.

In James chapter 1, James teaches us that God doesn't tempt with evil. He can't be tempted Himself; therefore, He tempts no one with evil things. Just as we grow to believe this truth, we should also believe He doesn't create bad things on the earth. Some may endure a bad situation and claim that God was testing or punishing them. This simply isn't how the Father operates. Scripture tells us we will face hardships and trail, but God isn't the source of those things.

To fully know the impact the fall had on humanity, we must know every bad circumstance is the direct effect of sin. The enemy roams the earth like a roaring lion, looking for someone to devour. Because sin has slipped into the world, the enemy now has access to scheme, tempt and manipulate us into sin. He is the root cause of all evil, not God.

Why Doesn't God Stop Bad Things?

I can't tell you why God didn't remove the sickness I desperately asked Him to remove from my siblings. I do believe there are things He does supernaturally prevent and things He allows to happen. When God doesn't stop bad situations from happening, they become opportunities for us to lean into His understanding. After both of my brothers passed, I accepted there was a reason He allowed those deaths to happen. As I accepted this, I pressed into Him. I'm so humbled by what He's created out of me in this process of trusting Him. He will work things out for the good of those who love Him. I know when something difficult is happening in my life, God's desire is restoration and justice.

We often look for supernatural miracles to confirm that God is real; even Christians do this. I believe God doesn't sometimes perform miracles because He knows that isn't what will increase our faith. He asks us to put our faith in His Son, not His miracles. In Luke chapter 16, we see the story of a rich man who finds himself in hades after he dies. He asks Abraham to send a message to his brothers to warn them what will happen if they don't believe in Jesus. Here is Abraham's response:

"He said to him, 'If they do not listen to Moses and the Prophets, they will not be convinced even if someone rises from the dead."

Luke 16:31

Abraham knew a miracle wouldn't provide them the faith they needed to believe. Those who seek miracles to confirm God is real will always seek miracles to confirm He is real. We believe through hearing the Word of God, not sight. (Romans 10:17) God is still doing miracles on the earth, but He isn't doing them to prove He is real. We put our faith and trust in the Gospel message to confirm in our hearts He is real.

Why Are Christians So Mean?

Many questions non-believers ask are a response to the misrepresentation of Jesus. We covered this in chapter 6 when we explored how to restore the reputation of the church; however, giving an apology doesn't answer why many Christians have misrepresented Jesus.

These questions often come from a deep wound. You may find through your conversations there is a past incident where someone was hurt that brought this question to the surface. As you speak with them, know the Holy Spirit can help you unveil these hurts and give you the truth to speak into their life. Having these questions answered will not give them the faith to believe. We want to answer them the best we can, but it is the hope of the Gospel they truly need. Answering this question and using it as an opportunity to unveil the truth may allow them to be more receptive to the Gospel.

In these conversations, I like to talk about the difference between living by grace and living by the law. Christians who are hurtful and cruel to non-believers have bought into lies about who God is and how He operates. Those who are judgmental believe the power of God's wrath has been passed to them to condemn the world. The good news is that God's wrath was poured out on His Son, so we didn't have to endure it. Anyone who hands out condemnation and judgement isn't operating in the likeness of Christ or under the influence of the Holy Spirit.

It's disheartening that many believers of Christ have inflicted wounds upon non-believers the way they have. Even so, these are my favorite conversations to explore. I'm confident when authentic believers are adamant about showing those who have been hurt a better way, we will see hard hearts soften and turn back to Him. We may not be able to answer this question for someone's specific experience, but we can always show them the true heart of God!

I'll ask those who have been hurt to share their experiences with me. This helps me understand their pain and allows the Holy Spirit to give me the truth to speak into their situation. We must attempt to empathize with their experience and apologize on behalf of the church. Sometimes an "I don't know" is an acceptable answer, but we must emphasize that what they experienced wasn't the nature of Jesus.

This list of questions is exhaustive. There are many questions that non-believers have regarding Christianity. I encourage you to discover more of those questions and take note of them when someone asks. You may even have some that you are aware of that I didn't mention. Always be diligent in seeking the answers and confirming what you believe. The Holy Spirit is an excellent guide and will help you use these questions to point to the answer the Gospel brings.

PROPHETIC WORDS

As we go from small conversations to meaningful encounters, we will need the Holy Spirit's help. Flowing in the prophetic is one of the most powerful ways we can connect people to the story of Jesus. The prophetic comes at various times and in any conversation. We should always be ready to hear from the Father and share His heart with others. I'm still learning much about the prophetic and how to operate in it, but I can share with you how it applies in sharing the Gospel with the lost.

Prophetic words are direct revelations from the Father that are supernaturally revealed to us. Many assume or believe only certain people can receive prophetic words. I promise you, it's for everyone! John 10: 27 says, "My sheep listen to my voice; I know them, and they follow me." We can all recognize the voice of God! This is a season He's sharing His voice and revelation to those listening. Let's be sure our ears are open with an intent to draw the lost closer to Him!

Hearing the voice of God starts in our secret places. I encourage you to pray and ask for these specific gifts as you spend time in His presence. Never stop asking that the gifts of prophecy will flow in your life. In situations where a non-believer can get bogged down with Christian jargon, the prophetic connects them to the Lord in supernatural ways. Let's look at some of these gifts and how they apply to your efforts in evangelism.

Words of Knowledge

Words of knowledge are ideas and thoughts the Lord reveals to us about situations and other people. They are usually pieces of information we shouldn't know. Often, these words will be a name, address or something else that can't be guessed. It's something small but impactful in someone's life. I was once given the name of someone's childhood friend who had passed and connected that to their current pain. These words will grab someone's attention to let them know there's a higher being wanting to speak to them through us! Shawn Bolz is a prophetic teacher who has been given an extreme gift in words of knowledge. I encourage you to explore some of his writings, such as *Translating God* and *Through the Eyes of Love.*

These words are often followed with another prophetic message. It may be a word that confirms something a person has been praying for or awakens a dream in their heart that they've forgotten. Connecting a lost person's heart to God through a word of knowledge can tune their ear to be receptive of what He will say next. We can't put words of knowledge in a box. When we are listening to an all-knowing God, the spectrum of knowledge we'll hear is vast. These prophetic words require a keen ear to the voice of God. They are usually very specific. It's vital to be in a healthy community where you can practice hearing and speaking the heart of God through these messages. With time, you will learn how to recognize the voice of God through them and share it with the lost!

One morning while running errands, The Lord gave me a word for a young lady working at the store I was at. He mentioned to me that this woman was hosting a party soon that she was very anxious about. I'll be honest, the Lord rarely gives me words like this, but I felt so compelled to share it. When I told the cashier what the Lord told me, she froze! She couldn't believe I knew that information. As I shared with her how I received it, the Lord also revealed to me she was anxious about some other areas of her life. I prayed for anxiety to be released off her before I left. Through one piece of information, the Lord made a way to break anxiety off her life. He wants to give you words of knowledge too!

Visions and Pictures

Visions and pictures are given to us exactly how they sound. They are images that relay a message about something. This is usually how the Lord reveals messages to me. It's a gift that has given me in-depth revelation over my life and allowed me to minister to others in powerful ways. This gift usually requires an interpretation, but not always. Sometimes you'll give someone an image and they'll know exactly what you are referring to. In my experience, these visions and pictures have been associated with an interpretation.

I was once ministering to a youth group, and the Lord revealed to me a picture for a teenager there. During the service, the Lord placed an image of a hen protecting her chicks into my mind for this teenage girl. After the service, I approached this young lady and prophesied over her about the image. She had desires for the small group she led to become like family, and I told her how the Lord had the same desires. I didn't know this young lady led a small group, but the Lord revealed this to me to share with her.

After I finished, she confessed she'd been doubting that she was an efficient leader. She used the phrase "terrible mother hen" to describe how she felt about her success to that group of girls. The image of the hen resonated with her because of her doubts that she was effective in leading this group. After I gave the image, I imparted truth and confidence about who she was in Jesus. This was a powerful moment of connection for this young lady as she heard the heart of God for her ministry.

Visions and pictures open avenues for truth and wisdom to be spoken into our lives, just as words of knowledge. The Lord imparts prophetic gifts upon us not only to connect His heart to believers, but to also use them in reaching the ones who are wandering.

Many non-believers have turned their ears from listening to Christians talk about their faith. But imagine if a lost person hears a stranger speaking of an image or vision about their life they shouldn't know about. It's the power of prophetic words that often grab someone's attention to hear the voice of God. We must learn to step in and connect the wanderer's heart to the main source. Visions and pictures are a beautiful way this happens.

Scripture

The Lord will often use scripture to speak in the prophetic as well. Sometimes, it will come after a word of knowledge or picture. Other times, it may not come with anything else. We should always be prepared by studying the Word of God. It's not only effective for our own lives, but it's such a powerful ministering tool when we can hear it and relay it for other people. There have been several occasions where the Lord has placed a scripture on my heart for someone and an interpretation on how it applied to their lives.

When I was just learning to hear the voice of God, I would often go walking late at night with my Bible to worship and pray. The Lord began revealing scriptures in my mind for certain individuals. One night, He gave me a verse that referenced producing fruit for the Kingdom. I had no interpretation for it, but I knew the Lord wanted me to send it to a certain couple He gave me an image of. They replied two days later with an awesome perspective on the scripture I had sent.

I didn't know the couple well, but they were having difficulty getting pregnant. They had recently been focusing on letting God use them where they were, even during their struggle. They felt the Lord was urging them to focus more on their spiritual fruit and trusting He would take care of helping them conceive. It was confirmation to them He was fighting their battle for them. From that word, they pressed into Him and focused on their spiritual journey with more confidence than before.

When believed, scripture captivates the hearts of His children. He uses His Word, just as the other gifts we've talked about, to allow us to set our attention on Him. I encourage you to pray for someone you love and ask the Lord to reveal a piece of His Word for you to share. Scripture tells us if we ask, we will receive. It's effective in connecting the hearts of the lost to Him as well! He wants to give us these prophetic gifts to grab the attention of those He loves. Be open to receive these heavenly messages and share them with those you meet!

These aren't all the ways the Lord uses the prophetic. A powerful resource for me in learning the different avenues of the prophetic was a book by David Edwards called *Activating a Prophetic Lifestyle*. It will empower you as well! I hope that you will explore the prophetic in your ministry and know His voice when He is speaking to you. When you can use what He's telling you to communicate His love to the lost, you'll see a more tangible fruit being produced from your ministry. You will also see His love piercing the heart of His children and the non-believer. In these moments, you know He is using you to connect His heart to the world!

WRAP UP

Evangelistic conversations can be daunting, but God made it a very simple thing to do. It's all about connecting His heart to the lost through our story and obedience to the Holy Spirit. It doesn't matter if you've been a Christian for six months or have a seminary degree, we all have a story effective for evangelism.

Sharing the Gospel is a humbling experience. So often, we won't know exactly what to say or how to answer a hard question, but the grace of God is enough. In the moments where we feel we are doomed to fail or mess up, He proves to us that we evangelize in His strength, not ours. I encourage you to practice. Always be intentional about learning through your experiences. The Holy Spirit is an excellent guide, but we want to be prepared and as ready as possible when opportunity arises!

So, you've shared the Gospel with someone, and they've turned their life over to Christ. What happens now?

As evangelists, it may not fall on our shoulders to disciple those we share the Gospel with, but with good practical knowledge, we can point them in a direction that will set them up to be discipled well! Let's discover what this looks like in the next chapter!

PRAYER FOR HEALING IN A TARGET PARKING LOT

The world is more receptive of the Gospel than many Christians tend to believe. Fear of rejection and worry over what to say have hindered me many times. As I've become more secure in my identity as a beloved daughter of God, I've grown in the confidence of having the Holy Spirit with me at all times. Knowing this truth makes it much easier to share my faith. One instance occurred around Christmas time in the middle of a busy store parking lot. As I made my way toward the entrance, I noticed a woman doing the same, but she was limping at a much slower pace. I sensed fresh compassion rise within my heart when I saw her. I approached the woman and began a conversation, explaining how I noticed her walking in pain. She confirmed her feet were causing the limp. I asked if I could pray for her. She shyly shook her head no (seemingly embarrassed that I offered). I explained that I believed in the power of prayer and that God was good and could heal her. To my surprise, she suddenly grabbed me close for a tight hug, crying and nodding the "okay" for me to pray for her. I held this beautiful woman in the middle of a busy Target parking lot and prayed boldly for the healing of her feet, but also for the pain she was carrying in her heart. I sensed she was carrying grief. I prayed as the Holy Spirit led, affirming her in the love of God and blessing her and her family in the name of Jesus. She wiped her tears and thanked me profusely. It was remarkable how quickly a denial for prayer turned into an encounter with the love of God. It reminded me that every time I stop to reach out to someone, God does what He does best; He meets people in the middle of their pain to bring hope and healing. "Christ in me, the hope of glory," is the answer for our aching world. I encourage you to take some risks from the security of knowing God-in-us is always receptive to those in need and able to meet them where they are at. With compassion and courage, we can boldly extend the good news that becomes the healing balm the world around us needs!

-Natalie

9

WHAT NEXT?

Now that we've covered some basics of evangelism, I want to use this chapter to touch on what happens next. It won't necessarily be our job to disciple new believers, but what we emphasize after someone accepts Christ is essential to the next phase of their walk. Whether it's with a random stranger or someone we have known for years, there are steps we should know to set new believers up for success in their spiritual walk. To be effective relational evangelists, we must connect new believers to relationship after they accept Christ. Sometimes, that might be you!

Learning to walk in Christ is a process. In our spiritual journeys, we go through seasons of hardship, joy, and renewal that teach us how to draw closer to the Father. What we initially teach a new believer after they accept

Christ will set them up for how they approach this process. Identity is of utmost importance as we guide the new believer through the next steps of the process.

We must emphasize identity to new believers, not so much the actions they should take. The authentic and faithful Christian has strong roots in who they have become in Christ, not what they do for Him. When we focus on service and action, we cause new believers to believe they must work to earn the gift they just received. When we focus on identity, we enforce that they are still recipients of this gift through their righteousness and oneness with Christ. Action and service will flow from this revelation of identity.

An intimate relationship with the Father is rooted in who He has created us to be. Some of us have relegated our relationship with Him to our works. We've often become accustomed to working for our salvation; for some, anything else seems foreign. The reason we enjoy working to gain our relationship is that we can control it. If we feel "distant" from God, we do things like ramp up our Bible study plan or find another team to join at church. Our identities are cemented in what Jesus did for us, not how well we practice our spiritual disciplines. If you don't know your relationship with the Father outside of your service, you need a fresh revelation of your identity in Him! Let's be sure we don't lead new Christians down this path of dead works. Let's go over some truths about identity you can talk with a new believer about.

YOUR OLD SELF WAS CRUCIFIED: ROMANS 6:6

When someone accepts Christ, a supernatural transformation takes place. New believers are immediately adopted into a family of righteousness. We may not tangibly feel that transition, but it happens just the same. When we receive the love of God through Christ, we become heirs to His Kingdom. In making us a part of this family, Jesus buried our old selves and destroyed our old desires and sin habits. This is often a truth that new believers have difficulty believing. We must emphasize this to them. Romans 6:6 claims,

"For we know that our old self was crucified with him so that the body ruled by sin might be done away with, that we should no longer be slaves to sin."

Romans 6:6

The love of Jesus eradicates the power of sin from our lives as He abolishes our past identities. We can't let it be acceptable for new believers to walk away from their conversion experience without being told this truth. For someone to fully walk as the righteousness of God, they must believe who they once were no longer exists. Many still struggle with sin because they don't believe this truth.

If we don't believe our old identities were crucified, we'll live according to a Gospel that forgives our past sins but doesn't have the power to address our future ones. If Jesus didn't die to demolish our old selves, He died in vain. There was already a way for God to forgive sin; through the sacrifice of animals. He didn't want to just eliminate that process of forgiveness, He wanted to eliminate the need for forgiveness altogether! The Lord hates sin because of how it corrupts our souls; therefore, He made a way for it to lose any power it had over us. We live by what we believe is true. Christians often get trapped in sin because they believe they're still sinners. New believers need to be renewed in their minds to this truth so they don't fall back into their old sinful patterns.

YOU ARE A NEW CREATION:
2 CORINTHIANS 5:17

When our past person is destroyed, someone new must take their place. After we tell believers their old nature was crucified, it's essential to explain the promise of their new identities in Christ. When someone believes that Jesus has removed their old nature, it creates space for them to listen to the Father about who they truly are in Him. We may not be able to tell new believers their destiny or purpose in building the Kingdom, but we can make them aware that through their new nature, they can discover them. Jesus wanted more than our sinful desires to be destroyed, He promised to create something beautiful and new within us! 2 Corinthians 5:17 says,

"Therefore, if anyone is in Christ, the new creation has come. The old has gone, the new is here!"

2 Corinthians 5:17

It's amazing to know God wants to turn us into someone new! A new joy will overwhelm us. New passions will arise, and we will see powerful things about ourselves that didn't exist before. Being aware of this new life will open our hearts and minds to dream about who Christ has made us. It changes everything about who we thought we were and gives us hope that we'll be better versions of ourselves. Christlike versions!

I'm still learning things about my new nature as I draw closer to the Father. Even though I've been a believer since I was seven, I am still seeing dead things from my past coming to life through the new man God has created in me. As I throw off lies that keep me trapped in my past, the Father is replacing those old areas with new passions and desires. We can never have revelations of who He has created us to be if we don't believe He has done a new work in us. Believe this promise about yourself and share it with new believers. God desires us all to thrive in our new identities!

YOU ARE A CHILD OF GOD: JOHN 1:12

When identities are affirmed in actions and spiritual disciplines, a master/servant relationship with God is presumed, but when our identities are found in who we are and not what we do, we discover that God finds delight in calling us sons and daughters. In a society running rampant with fatherless homes, this may be a hard concept for some to believe. I've met individuals who resent the relationships they have with their parents, so the truth that God calls them a child is difficult to fathom.

The reason some find it hard to believe in this father/son relationship between believer and God is because they feel they don't deserve it. The question we all face in our spiritual walks is, "Does God really love me?" We question God's love for us when we feel we don't deserve it. Through the sacrifice Christ made on the cross, we've been "given the right" (John 1:12) to be the children of God. According to our old nature, we don't deserve the status of son or daughter; however, as the righteousness of God, He made a way for us to inherit the Kingdom as His children.

God as my Father was a concept I'd always heard but didn't believe until recently. Most of my life I have lived as an orphan. I was simply a slave to the service and duty of my ministry. Learning to walk as a son has been the most humbling and empowering journey of my life. I discovered who my Father was and how He viewed me as His child. It's our ministry of reconciliation that enables us to bring new believers into this truth about their inheritance as children of God as well!

As you speak with a new believer, it is crucial to emphasize this new identity as a child of God. Use verbiage including words or phrases like son/daughter, child, and Father. Stay away from words like serve, responsibility, and duty. Those are important, but they will flow from our revelations as children of God. The language you use during the conversion experience for a new believer can put them on a trajectory that sets them up to take on the role of a servant or child of God! We are servants of Christ, but we're children first!

ACCESS TO THE FATHER

In chapter one, I spoke of reconciliation and how it was the Father's ultimate plan all along. As we communicate truth and identity to the new believer, it's also essential for us to communicate the access we now have to the Father. These forms of access are well known to believers, but they have often been communicated as religious disciplines. We have passed them onto new believers as duties we "ought to do" instead of opportunities for building a relationship with our Father. When we understand that these avenues draw us into intimacy with God, we will see and experience aspects of His love that can't be accessed through religious duty alone. We should present these disciplines to new believers with the right understanding of their purpose.

Prayer Life

How often we pray is a good indicator of how much we truly believe in its power. In the last chapter, we will talk about how an active pursuit in prayer is essential for the evangelistic lifestyle. Here, I want to discuss the importance of showing the new believer the value of a persistent prayer life.

Children are adorable prayers. They are powerful as well! There's supernatural power in "child-like" faith. If you ever listen to a child pray, you'll notice their prayers lack one thing: themselves. They pray for their friends that are sick, their parents or their pet turtle, Henry. Praise, thanksgiving, and intercession are very common during a child's prayer. At a young age, you aren't very aware of your own needs. The older we get, the more we notice ourselves, and our prayers become a little more self-centered.

As we get older, our prayer life can easily turn into a plea of desperation or a quick avenue for repentance. We hit our knees when times are hard or when we're convicted of something we have done. When we see prayer as a means of communication to receive rather than give, we rob ourselves and the Father of the intimacy that prayer should provoke. We must teach the new believer that prayer is more than a petition to have our desires met. Prayer is an intimate form of communication that allows us to honor Him, thank Him and intercede for powerful things to happen in the lives of others.

Prayer is also an opportunity for us to listen to the Father's voice. I think about the comment boxes many restaurants have in their lobbies. After you fill out a card and drop it in the box, you walk away with the small chance you will ever hear from anyone regarding your comment. Using prayer to get what we want is our proverbial way of dropping a note in the comment box and walking away. It would be more effective if we took our complaint to a manager and listened to their input directly. Show the new believer the value of listening to the Father in moments of prayer. You will teach them how to walk away with a clearer direction and the Father's side of the story. Prayer goes two ways. If new believers aren't taught this, they will end up talking without receiving insight or knowledge from the Lord!

Reading Scripture

Reading scripture takes discipline. The Word of God includes every aspect of His character and sheds light on who we are in Him. Reading scripture allows us to know Him intimately. Those who read scripture to know God instead of to pursue knowledge can't get enough of their Bible. It's invigorating reading the Bible when it comes alive to you. When you ask a new believer to read their Bible, reiterate how it isn't a responsibility, but an honor and privilege to see the heart of God within its pages. Reading the Bible for a new believer will bring many revelations about Jesus to their mind and soul. If they're taught to read it just for knowledge sake, they will eventually get bored and put it down.

We should teach believers to read scripture from the lens of the resurrected Jesus. Seeing the Bible in this light allows it to come alive to us. Reading and meditating on God's Word is the primary way He speaks to us and injects His love into our souls. We don't read scripture to know about God; we read scripture to KNOW God. As we teach believers about reading the Bible, the way we teach them to read it is paramount. We can teach them to read it so it produces new life within them, or we can teach them to read it in a way that produces dead works. It's vital we teach them the difference.

Worship

This is my favorite way of hearing from the Lord. We all have different ideas about what worship entails. My definition of worship is very simple. It's, "living a life that gives the highest worth to a single person or thing." We tend to relegate worship to a Sunday morning experience, but anytime we take a moment to thank Him for His goodness, give unto His name or simply show His love to someone else, we are worshipping Him.

For this book and the topic at hand, I want to focus on the intentional moments we set aside just for worship. Worship takes place on Sundays, but even more so, it happens in our secret places. I'm not referring to your daily Bible reading plan or devotion time. We must teach new believers how to seek His presence in those dedicated moments to be with Him and give Him honor.

We teach new believers how to pursue these moments because they are where revelations of Christ happen. The Lord does a tremendous work on our hearts in the time we delegate to worship Him. I believe it's important for new believers to develop a hunger for the Lord in worship early in their walk. When believers intentionally seek the Spirit of God, their spiritual maturity and fruit grow exponentially. The sooner we develop the desire to be with God in our secret places, the less of an opportunity we give other motives and desires to creep into our hearts.

Let's tell new believers how to seek these special moments, but let's show them as well. Invite someone you have led to Christ into these moments with you. Get together to pray and worship. Show them what you do and why you do it. As the Lord captivates their hearts and transforms their lives in these intimate places, they'll pursue Him on a deeper level on their own. Teach them that the access they have to the Father in these moments is available at work, home, and everywhere else they go. It's from our secret place of worship that a true lifestyle of love and compassion flows. We must teach new believers the value of worship as an avenue to intimacy with the Father.

Everything that has been discussed in this chapter doesn't fall on you. It's not feasible to discuss all these aspects to someone who has just received Christ, especially if you have met them in a random place, but we should know these aspects to teach new believers what we can. As relational evangelists, many conversions we have will be with ones we already have relationships with. That doesn't mean we won't have time to share some of these things during the evangelistic opportunities we receive on the go. It just means we must be aware of what happens next in those situations.

I place a high value on getting believers plugged into the local church. As evangelical Christians, it's our responsibility to point new believers in the right direction.

We should never leave them trying to figure things out on their own. Next, we will discuss how to move forward in both random and relational conversations.

FOLLOWING UP - THE RANDOM CONVERSATIONS

The other night, while having dinner at a restaurant, I began conversing with a gentleman working there. I wanted to share the Gospel with him, but through our conversation, he revealed that he was already a believer. We talked for a while, and I prayed with him. As I was leaving, I asked him if I could connect with him on social media. He added me on Facebook right away.

I enjoy following people I meet on social media. It gives me instant access to their lives. Whether or not someone accepts the Lord, we should always ask to connect on social media or get a phone number. If you have loved well and they feel you genuinely care for them, they'll appreciate the new connection. This doesn't mean that we can bombard our new friend with messages about Jesus. We should use tact in how we interact with them. Facebook or Instagram are great ways to stay connected with those you meet. Another opportunity may arise through this outlet, but don't force anything.

It's always acceptable to invite people you meet randomly to come to church with you. If you get into a spiritual conversation, invite them to a service or small group meeting. They may not have accepted Jesus, and that's okay. Sometimes it takes multiple interactions or coming to a church service for someone to entertain a relationship with the Lord. If they say no, get their number with an intention to ask them to coffee later. Sometimes you must be patient. Take your time and just build the relationship if you are given the opportunity to. You should be able to get a good idea if they are interested in seeing or speaking with you again.

If you meet someone randomly and they accept the Lord during your conversation, always give them access to you. Since you were used to lead them in accepting Christ, they may lean on you heavily early in their walk. Be intentional about meeting up with them if they live nearby or help point them toward a good discipleship community. If you invite them to your church and they decide they don't want to go there, nothing is wrong with that. Help them find a church in the area where they can grow in their new journey. You can still meet with them to talk about what the Lord is doing in their life. They may be someone you run with for a long time, or they may find another mentor or group of believers to run with. Make yourself available. That's one important aspect of relational evangelism.

After conversion, Christians need connection with

other believers. You may be that connection, or it may be your responsibility to point them toward another group who can disciple them. In a world where everyone interacts so closely, we can't accept that our evangelism stops at conversion or rejection. We can build a relationship and connect with them on the premise of our love for them. Be intentional about connecting and following up!

FOLLOWING UP - THE WELL-KNOWN CONVERSATIONS

This one applies to all of us. It's not rare to share the Gospel with someone you already know. This evangelism happens most often in places such as work and school. They can also happen within the circles of friends we have outside of the church. None-the-less, they are evangelistic opportunities with people we already know. So, what's next when a good friend or acquaintance accepts Jesus?

When you lead someone you know to Christ, it's a powerful testament to your integrity. Those who know you see aspects of your character. Over time they may even see your fleshly nature. If someone you know receives Christ after you share the Gospel with them, it means they see something in you they find appealing. They see Jesus in you, and they want what you have. Kudos! Close friends can often be the hardest people to share the Gospel with.

147

Since you'll see this new believer often, you carry a bigger responsibility. Many aspects we talked about with random conversations still apply here. Invite them to church and stay connected with them. It will be very tempting for you to overwhelm them with conversations about Jesus. Be patient and tactful with this relationship. Just be available. If they cling to you and are eager to learn from you, run with it. If they seem resistant, be available and gracious to them. The last thing you want to do is make the situation awkward or give them a reason to resent you.

In time, talk with them about the areas we spoke of earlier in the chapter. Since you will see them around, it's good to engage in conversation and speak their new identities over them. Someone who accepts Christ is now on a journey of transformation. Remember that they will change and grow just as you are. It's unfair to put certain expectations on them. They may find some other Christians to do life with or may not be interested in coming to your church. Nothing is wrong with that. Just know you have been obedient to your role. It's a positive thing they are joining a community; celebrate with them in that. Still, honor and pursue your relationship with them. That doesn't change if they go a different way.

There's so much that happens after someone accepts Christ. It's a brand-new life to navigate! Even though what happens after conversion isn't solely our responsibility, I believe we can set someone up to thrive when we connect with them and teach them about their identities. Every situation is different. You'll find practical ways of connecting that work for you. Just as the Lord has led you in sharing the Gospel, He will guide you in connecting with a new believer. Trust He will use you to set them up well for their journey with Him!

10

LIVING THE EVANGELISTIC LIFESTYLE

We've covered a lot of ground on this topic of evangelism. I pray this book has given you the confidence to believe you are a powerful messenger of the Gospel. I believe we are seeing a wave of evangelists being raised in our country for such a time as this. In a consumerist society that has seen a "come and see" church dynamic erupt, I hope to see individuals step into their evangelistic callings and be equipped to go and tell.

Evangelism is a calling we all have. You may not have a desire to preach on the streets, but you've been given unique abilities to share the Gospel where you are. We haven't just been called to evangelize; evangelism is a lifestyle we've been asked to live. Living an evangelistic lifestyle requires some things from us I want to cover before we bring this book to a close.

In my earlier years, some may have labeled me selfish. My lifestyle was self-centered, to say the least. When I helped someone, it usually came with an agenda to get something in return. I cared very little for those around me and would use anyone to get the things I wanted. I praise the Lord that He has brought my new identity to the surface. He is still working on my heart in many areas, but I've found a constant stream of joy being able to give and serve people. We can't fully walk in a lifestyle of evangelism when we put ourselves first. Selfishness hinders us from sharing the Gospel out of compassion and love for the lost. To be an effective evangelist, you must have a heart of humility.

HUMILITY

Putting others before ourselves is an essential aspect of humility, but we first must obtain the humility of standing before the Lord and identifying our worth in His presence. With Him, we are everything, but without Him, we are nothing. This revelation of humility will drench our character with selflessness and compel us to evangelize with no other agenda. To live an evangelistic lifestyle, we must always seek humility before the Lord. When we evangelize from any place other than humility, sharing the Gospel becomes self-centered and driven with false motives. Proverbs 11:2 says,

"When pride comes, then comes disgrace, but with humility comes wisdom."

Proverbs 11:2

Humility is the gateway to wisdom, and pride leads to disgrace. Wisdom is necessary for sharing the Gospel. There will be situations and conversations where we will need wisdom to express what God wants to say. We will never receive this wisdom when our hearts are full of pride; only humility will open the door to receive it. As you learn to walk in humility, wisdom will be your friend. We all need wisdom when making decisions and navigating situations in our lives. An evangelistic lifestyle covered in humility will allow us to hear and receive this supernatural wisdom straight from heaven.

As much as we may desire it, we can't "will" ourselves to have humility; we can't just make it happen. It's a characteristic that flows right from the heart of God. Posturing our hearts before the Lord and reflecting on the Gospel message is the only way we receive genuine humility. Losing our worth in the presence of God is what transforms us and aligns our hearts with His. If you find you have difficulty putting yourself aside, spend time with Him, asking Him for a revelation of how big He is and how small you are. Only when we do this, can we drop our agendas in evangelism and center on His.

COMPASSION

Every decision Jesus made was out of His compassion for people. Compassion is a by-product of humility, and just the same, fills our hearts as we spend time in the presence of the Lord. Living a lifestyle of evangelism requires a constant pursuit for more compassion. As we adopt His compassion for people, we will see and love them how He does. Our compassion for people is the driving force of authentic evangelism.

Compassion is a supernatural gift; therefore, there are supernatural implications when we share the Gospel with compassion. Have you ever confided in someone and they empathized and cared for you in a way you couldn't explain? Compassion has that effect on our relationships. It's a direct avenue of love from the Father that pierces the heart in unexplainable ways. If we lack compassion, our evangelistic lifestyle will lack the true heart of the Lord for His people.

When we love someone from a place of compassion, we are fully in the moment. It has no expectations. We can't predict the future and limit our compassion based on an assumption. It also has no record of the past. Compassion allows us to empathize with people where they are and share the Gospel accordingly. Making this a lifestyle requires us to be fully present in our interactions, with no record of wrongs or false assumptions. This is how Jesus ministered. We should desire to follow in His footsteps.

INTEGRITY

As an evangelist, fighting for our integrity is non-negotiable. We carry a message of holiness and purity. If people see we live a lifestyle that doesn't reflect either of these, they'll see our message as flawed. I often reflect on what it would look like if Jesus gave into temptation in the desert. I know this point is moot, but would He have carried a message that people found hope in, or would His sin have caused him to lose His voice and influence over those who followed Him?

When I say we must fight for our integrity, we must fight. I'll attest, there have been times my integrity has taken a hit due to a lack of wisdom in my decision making. Striving for holiness is difficult, but with the help of Jesus as our high priest, it's essential to give integrity top priority in our lives. The Lord values integrity because He died to remove our sinful nature. He desires to see carriers of His Gospel walking and living in the identity He sacrificed Himself for them to have.

Truthfully, your integrity isn't for you. It's for those you have influence over. Many Christians have deep wounds because those they followed didn't value integrity in their lives. Christian leaders have fallen into sexual immorality, fraud, and other sinful habits and have left those that followed them lacking faith and credibility in the Gospel message. Many followers have even left the church and the faith due to such instances. We should value integrity because we value the work the Lord is doing through us for others. We fight for it because those we influence are counting on us to be followers of the Lord who walk in holiness and purity.

SPIRITUAL DISCIPLINES

An evangelistic lifestyle is one of constant growth and communication with the Father. Praying, going to church or reading scripture aren't things that we always enjoy doing. That's where discipline comes in. Spiritual disciplines often cause tension because we feel we should always want to do them when we don't. God, however, honors our sacrifice and commitment to growing through His Word, praying and spending time with Him in worship. Let's explore these areas and how they pertain to us. Evangelistic lifestyles require us to flow in these disciplines daily. By practicing them, we become intimate with the Lord and bend an ear to hear what He longs to share with us.

Persistent Prayer

Alvin Reid says it best, "Before we can talk to people about God, we must talk to God about people." Jesus was an avid prayer. He would wake up earlier than anyone else and go to His secret place to talk with the Father. I like to believe that He was talking to Him about me! Scripture tells us He is still at the right hand of the Father interceding for us. He is constantly communicating with the Father about you and me!

Evangelism requires us to soak our entire lives in prayer. A life of prayer goes much further than a couple of conversations a day with the Lord. It requires us to be in constant communication with the Father. As we walk into a coffee shop, we are praying for those there and how the Lord wants us to minister. Wherever we go, we are communicating with the Lord about how He wants to use us and what He wants us to say. Scripture tells us to not worry about anything but pray about everything. I don't believe we can take this command lightly. We should be in prayer about all areas of our lives.

The amazing thing about soaking our lives in prayer is that it increases our expectancy for our prayers to be answered. It elevates our faith to speak to someone and share the story of Jesus with them. I believe that how often we pray is a direct indicator of how much we believe in its power. Praying allows us to hear from the Lord. When we make it a part of our lifestyle, hearing from the Lord also becomes a part of our lifestyle, not just an "every-once-in-a-while" thing!

Saturating in God's Word

It's impossible to tell the story of Jesus if you don't know the story of Jesus. Every verse we read (even in the Old Testament) points directly to Him. We should dwell on the things He has said and the promises He spoke in scripture. The more we understand what scripture says, the better we can connect others to the heart of God.

The Father is longing to speak with you. He wants to share His heart with you through His Word. As we saturate our hearts and minds in the Word of God, we become more confident in our ability to share His heart with the world. The Bible is fresh with revelation every time you read its contents. God's Word is a powerful way that He drenches us with His love and compassion! It's so alive and active! The lost will see this love and compassion in addition to our confidence in scripture. As they notice these things about us, it will open them up to receive the message of good news we are preaching.

God's Word never returns void. The more we know Him through His Word, the more we can speak life into those we meet. It pierces and shifts atmospheres when we speak the truth of scripture. We must make spending time in it a part of our everyday lives.

Worship

Worship is the constant practice of giving God the honor

and worth He deserves. Authentic evangelists have an ever-present awareness of His goodness and hunger to share it with the world. Worship doesn't just relegate itself to a Sunday experience, worship happens in our cars, at our jobs, and in our homes. As we declare the worth of the Lord, we are filled with hope that He desires to do abundant things in those we encounter. When worship becomes a part of our lives, we learn to see the power of what the Lord is doing, even in the most helpless situations.

To see a good example of someone who made worship a part of his lifestyle, I encourage you to look into the life and writings of David. He's known as the man after God's own heart. His life was a sacrifice of praise and adoration to the Lord. Even in his mistakes and times of fear and anxiety, he looked to the comfort of the Lord through his worship to Him. Learning to praise and worship the Lord changes our perspective to evangelize. Adoring and reflecting on the goodness of the Lord allows us to see His love is for everyone. He longs to restore the lost through our evangelistic lifestyles.

WRAP UP

The evangelistic lifestyle is hard and takes sacrifice. It's not one of comfort or convenience. Luke 9:23 Jesus proclaims, "Whoever wants to be my disciple must deny themselves and take up their cross daily and follow me." I look to someone like Paul as someone who lived what it looked like to carry his cross daily. He lived this radically!

As believers dedicated to spreading the Gospel, we must ask ourselves what carrying our crosses daily requires from us. Some of us haven't learned what that means for our lives just yet. Are you one that I mentioned earlier who accepted Christ and dropped your cross because you thought you had done all you needed to do to be saved? If you think this might be you, I urge you to ask what you'll need to sacrifice to pick it back up and carry it for the sake of sharing the Gospel!

Navigating what this sacrifice looks like is different for all of us. You may never be asked to give up your life, ministry or family for the Gospel, but there is always something we should let go of if asked. The question is, are you willing? The evangelistic lifestyle requires us to wrestle with these questions. Ask yourself what's in your way of pursuing the Gospel. Are you willing to part with it so you can live a radical life of evangelism?

Living the evangelistic lifestyle compels us to make sharing the Gospel our key priority. When you walk into a grocery store, how are you expecting to build the Kingdom? When you meet a lost friend for lunch, how are you praying that the Lord will use you to speak truth into their life? Through prayer, boldness, and expectancy, everything we do is ripe for sharing the Gospel. We are always aware of opportunities, and every situation becomes a moment of evangelism. We live, eat and breathe sharing the Gospel. This is the evangelistic lifestyle.

We must also know how our Gospel story is changing. Our story becomes one of many twists and layers. We must learn to apply every situation to the cross. When everything in our lives is filtered through the Gospel, our entire life becomes useful in speaking hope and life to non-believers. The Gospel doesn't just refer to our conversion experience. It saved us, and it's essential for every aspect of our lives. Living this lifestyle allows us to see the Gospel alive and active in every situation. It gives us the confidence to speak the life of Jesus back into every dead thing!

I pray that as you have read this book, a stirring in your heart has taken place to evangelize to the lost. What we've covered has hopefully been empowering in giving perspective and useful tools for evangelizing. I encourage you to keep pursuing the Gospel. Reflect daily on how it applies to your life and pursue the evangelistic lifestyle that gives your story the most leverage for transformation. Continue to learn and grow in your evangelistic calling. As you gain experience and reflect on your own Gospel story, I know you will become the hell shaking evangelist the Lord has created you to be!

It has been my pleasure to share my heart on evangelism with you. Run your race well and never stop your efforts in sharing the Gospel message. I believe we're on the brink of seeing revival breakout in our nation, and it starts with evangelists just like you and me! You are the evangelist your community needs. Your story is powerful to bring hope and salvation to the lives all around you. Go tell it!

BIRTHING A STRIP CLUB MINISTRY

Our city hosts a "festival-style" event downtown on the first Friday of every month. Our youth ministry knew there would be people from all walks of life out that night, so we were planning on gathering to share the Gospel with anyone we could. I was running a little late, so as I spotted some of my people chatting with a group, I quickly parked nearby so I could join. At this point in my life, I was serving in youth ministry and working with our church's homeless outreach ministry. Evangelism was a top gifting in my life, and I was eager to get out among the crowds to talk about Jesus!

As I made a beeline for my group, I noticed an older woman talking with a burly man outside the entrance of a strip club. My heart started pounding. I knew this was the Holy Spirit stirring me to start a conversation with her. I kept trying to talk myself out of it, but the nudging of the Spirit to speak to her was growing stronger by the second.

I stopped, "Uhm, hey there! I'm just out with a group from my church tonight, seeing if anyone needs prayer." I knew this could get awkward!

The woman nodded.

"So, do you work here?" I asked.

She nodded again and said she managed the girls dancing inside. She and the man standing next to her glanced at each other, then he took off on his motorcycle.

Unprepared and overly excited, I blurted out, "Well, um, I'd love to have a relationship with your girls!" She took a long drag on her cigarette and kept staring at me. "I mean, I'd love to help in any way that I can."

I was trying to backtrack from the obvious creepy way I came across about my intentions with the girls. "I am just wondering if the girls working here might have any needs that I could try to help with. Do you all need water bottles? Snacks? Anything at all?"

Food relief was the area of ministry I was accustomed to helping with, so naturally, I kept asking if they had any food requests. I could tell she was thinking about my idea. She let me know the ladies working there had specific needs for feminine hygiene products. She explained they constantly asked her for them, but she no longer needed to carry them in her older age.

Again, with an eager tone, I responded, "I have so many!" (Thinking of the stocked warehouse for our homeless ministry, not my personal stock at home!) "When can I bring them to you?" She gave me a time and date for the following week.

I felt like I was floating for the rest of the weekend! I couldn't wait to tell my boss, other pastors, and friends about this newfound opportunity God had opened for us. With the help and release from my boss, I quickly gathered a small team of women and two men to help us with the delivery. We loaded up feminine hygiene products, roses, and chocolate for the girls working at this club.

I had no pre-conceived plan for the drop off that day. I wanted the Lord to lead. It couldn't have gone any better! The bouncer and the manager let us gather with the girls to pray over them during business hours! They agreed that our team could come back when needed. Of course, "when needed" for me became every single holiday or any reason I could think of to go! Every time we went, we got more open with the girls in prayer, asking them about their faith and what they believed about Jesus.

After three years of monthly visits, these girls began affectionately referring to us as "the church ladies." We told them many times that these special names for us made us feel silly, but we could tell this was their way of showing love back to us. By this point, they seemed to know we weren't there to have religious exchanges with them. We wanted to know everything about them and encourage their sense of dreaming again. It was our intention, every time we met, to remind them they were not forgotten, and they had a Father in Heaven who would do anything to pursue them with His love and kindness.

One day it happened! Easter of 2013, two of the women from the club gave their lives to Jesus! Through one of the girl's radical transformations, she connected us with two other local strip clubs and a nearby bar that employed women bartenders. She became the evangelist! Her dream was to own a big van so she could pick up all her friends for church on Sunday mornings.

This new opportunity of sharing God's love, the Gospel, and helping meet physical needs began penetrating light into the dark atmosphere of these clubs. These girls were coming to Christ! Bartenders were getting in touch with their emotions after years of dismissing their trauma. Bouncers were even speaking life and truth to the women in the clubs in ways that could only be attributed to God's intervention. We saw these women value each other in ways not cultivated before. Of course, there were still hard moments. Girls still cycled back to drugs and stripping. They struggled with financial instability and the lure of false promises that the sex industry offers.

This is what changed me through the process: God's character became clearer to me as I worked closely among the brokenness in these girls' lives. Lamentations 3:22 states that, "the steadfast love of the Lord never ceases." This great patience from God and His desire to be long-suffering with us changed my heart and mind in my time of walking with these women.

Evangelism isn't a transaction or exchange from people to pray a methodical prayer. Those moments of decision have their place, but one's choosing of Christ is a choice that transforms their entire lives. It's a decision that we make because God loved us first, giving us the ability to lay down our lives in fresh surrender to Him daily. We become inflamed with His passion for other people by that same love. Let's not let anything hinder the stoking of that fire in our hearts.

-Haley

Thank you

A simple thank you to all who helped me process, write and publish this book. Many of you believed in me and pushed me in the moments I wanted to give up the most. To God be the glory and may we all be better evangelists as a result of this team effort. I love you all!

ABOUT THE AUTHOR

Mitchell Johnson currently works full-time for the largest burn center in the United States. Although he has spent several years in ministry, much of Mitchell's career has been spent in the workforce with various companies. He has a bachelor's degree in Sports Management and has worked in numerous leadership roles throughout his career. He desires to see the Gospel being advanced, not only through the local church, but through Christians stepping into their evangelistic callings in the workplace.

Throughout his time in ministry, Mitchell has noticed a dire need to emphasize authentic relationships in evangelism and discipleship. His hope is that through his lifestyle of faith and relational connection, he can help point the broken world back to Jesus. He longs to equip others to pursue their callings in evangelism and empower them to step into their identity as powerful advocates for the Lord.

Mitchell is a native of Augusta, Ga where he has lived since the age of seven. In his spare time, you can find him watching the Chicago Cubs, playing with Legos or exploring new ideas on his laptop. He enjoys grinding his own coffee beans and has a secret desire of opening his own coffee shop and bookstore when he retires.

www.pursuingthegospel.com

Made in the USA
Monee, IL
16 April 2020